Healing Earthquakes

A LOVE STORY

IN POEMS

Jimmy Santiago Baca

Grove Press   New York

Copyright © 2001 by Jimmy Santiago Baca

Published simultaneously in Canada
Printed in the United States of America

Some of these poems have appeared in the Whitney Museum, New York, with James Drake's photographic exhibition, Watershed Anthology, University of Wisconsin-La Crosse, and the *Walking Rain Review*

Library of Congress Cataloging-in-Publication Data

Baca, Jimmy Santiago, 1952–
    Healing earthquakes : a love story in poems / Jimmy Santiago Baca.
        p.   cm.
    ISBN 0-8021-3814-4
    1. Love poetry, American.   I. Title.
    PS3552.A254 H43 2001
    811'.54—dc21   00-068169

DESIGN BY LAURA HAMMOND HOUGH

Grove Press
841 Broadway
New York, NY 10003

01 02 03 04   10 9 8 7 6 5 4 3 2

For Stacy J.,
this poet's dream of beauty, love and compassion.
All these love poems are the only gifts
I can offer to someone as beautiful as you,
and may as many blessings as the
Sun and Moon give to the seasons, be yours as well,
as your soul journeys in the dance
that will merge your sweet heart
with your great loving vision . . .
I honor you woman, so dance! dance! dance!

Acknowledgments

I would like to thank the gifted poet Efren Lopez, a true jaguar warrior, for helping me edit and put *Healing Earthquakes* together; his encouragement, support and friendship were indispensable in making this book a reality. To Karina Oliva, for tirelessly working for weeks, typing and retyping the poems and offering her insightful suggestions. And my deepest gratitude to my kids—their love and honesty keeps my life an incredibly rich journey.

Book I

As Life Was

One

With this letter I received from a young Chicano
doing time in New Boston, Texas,
    I'm reminded of the beauty of bars
    and how my soul squeezed through them
    like blue cornmeal through a sifting screen
    to mix with the heat and moisture of the day
    in each leaf and sun ray
        offering myself
        to life like bread.
He tells me he reads a lot of books and wants my advice
and more amazed
    he quotes from my books, honoring my words
    as words that released him from the bars,
    the darkness, the violence of prison.
It makes me wonder,
    getting down on myself as I usually do,
    that maybe I'm not the pain in the butt
        I sometimes think I am.
I used to party a lot, but now I study landscapes
and wonder a lot,
    listen to people and wonder a lot,
    take a sip of good wine and wonder more,
    until my wondering has filled five or six years
    and literary critics and fans
        and fellow writers ask
    why haven't you written anything in six years?
And I wonder about that—
    I don't reveal to them
    that I have boxes of unpublished poems

and that I rise at six-thirty each morning
    and read books, jot down notes,
    compose a poem,
        throwing what I've written or wondered
        on notepads in a stack in a box
                    in a closet.
Filled with wonder at the life I'm living,
distracted by presidential impeachment hearings
        and dick-sucking interns and Iraq bombings,
my attention is caught by the kid
without a T-shirt in winter
on the courts who can shoot threes and never miss,
by a woman who called me the other night
threatening to cut her wrists because she was in love
    and didn't want to be in love,
by the crackhead collecting cans at dawn along the freeway.
    Sore-hearted at the end of each day,
    wondering how to pay bills,
        thinking how I'll write a poem
    to orphans for Christmas
    and tell them that's their present
    and watch them screw up their faces—
    saying, huh,
        wondering what kind of wondering fool
        I've become
    that even during Christmas I'm wondering . . .
    caught in the magical wonder
    of angels on Christmas trees
        colored lightbulbs
all of it making me remember the awe and innocence
    of my own childhood,
        when Santa came with a red bag
        to the orphanage
            and gave us stockings
            bulging with fruit and nuts.
It was a time of innocence, gods walking around my bunk
        at night,

divine guardians whispering at my ear
how they'd take care of me—
and they did, armies of angels have attended me
in rebellious travels,
and the only thing that's changed since then
is instead of me waiting for Santa,
I'm like an ornery pit bull leashed to a neck chain
aching to bite the ass of an IRS agent
wondering why anyone in their right mind would,
with only one life to live, have a job making people so miserable.
It's something to wonder about.

Two

Now rises this poet's soul
from an unmarked grave in the middle of nowhere—
two sticks wired together, hammered deep
into the drought-stricken dirt.
At the base a mound of rocks.
The image of my life
after having fought every inch of the way
for dignity and meaning
to be out here in stinging dust blizzards
and scrabble scrub brush—
my soul
raises itself into a blazed howl
and crusty stalk in too much hurt
and instant glory
that gives meaning to the hard struggle
and deep-seeing journey
of my soul—
and who is the poet?
*   *   *

He works with no more magic than you or I,
he is not swept away by a woman's trailing skirt
or a man's scraped fist, nor does he need pale language to
    tell of love—
dirty sheets, stale morning city air, loneliness
are words he uses.
            Each act is a ritual, and if the ritual does not act,
            if the candles, spice, fire, incense do not work,
            blow them all out,
        take words, true good words, and open the door and
            sing to the night,
        let it be known that one man, one bare, scraggly, leaf-
            voiced
        man, sings his words as dear and true
        as does the arroyo its dust and gully rain.
His words lay tracks the rain follows pours down and expresses
    itself in.
His words give loam young roots can fatten in.
His words strip sashaying silk from emotions
and show you what love is,
what love is—
            the universe of a gutted bull
            its veined belly resembling a planet.
Here, point out the eye of the bull, that mean, glowing sun,
the world orbits around.
Tell the language of bells in its throat, the deafening signs of
    eternal language
in its horns. Tell it.
            And let others cry foul, how your words and temper
            wound them. Let them.
My poetry—
no shadows cling to its coat,
and in its pocket there is only a hand, and a few seeds
spread across the ground I walk.
What blossoms I won't pluck for myself
I leave them for others and go on,

my gift is merely the day,
and there is no room for anything else
but a human enjoying his lifework.

My poetry offers no room for anything else.
It is as clear to me now as when my mind
first shook with images,
bathed in realization that
I could work out a life no matter
how crooked the path had been left,
I could straighten it out, turn for turn,
mile for mile.

Those who took it the first time
became saints, lords, lovers and rebels,
the rest of us, delaying ourselves
alongside the road,
lift stones in our hands for protection,
cleave to the earth
cloaked in the dream light of our sleep.

I wake up, realizing I am one of the dreamers,
and I arise unnamed, shaggy-hearted,
a brave bison
pounding out poems in my lonely exile
against the rock;
passing the stinking carcasses of my fellows,
their hearts wrenched out
for gold,
the plains dotted black with empty eyes.
I bellow my vulgar dismay
and shake my horns at the pale face of death,
its long blond hair screaming in the wind
as I paw my soul for words
and rush with wild, reddened eyes,
shuddering the ground,

thundering at the footing of delicate built words,
tearing through the page,
my breath burning, burning it . . .

Three

My poems go out to the working people
in Grants' mines, to the farmers in Socorro
and Belén: my poems are *ristras* drying on rooftops—
the long red chili strands
strung together and knotted at the stems.
The wind rattles them
and the seeds inside the pods
shake coldly.
I think of my heart—
dry and crackly, the dry seeds of dreams
rasping against the tough red inner skin.

My poems have rubbed themselves
on the fingers of a young girl who then rubbed her eyes
and wept all night
in her bedroom for a lover.
From birth my tongue has had a fire
for communication
with trees and dirt and water,

for homes in my barrio
that sniff the ground for something lost.
Kids cling together like leaves on a branch
grown from the earth
outside dripping faucets.

The pictures of my grandfather,
now dead, hold in his eyes the ancient song

of wild drum, and in the eyes of my father,
now dead, the ruins of red dreams.

In winter the barrio stirs quietly,
its ways soft, like an animal sensing
the wind's heart,
flickers
red ashes in wood stoves,
keeping the warm fire alive.

I go looking for poems,
I walk past the church, then back up
and climb up the steps to the landing
and look in. An old man kneels in front
of *La Virgen*, beckoning her to remove
the boulder from his heart. I lean
against the great doors watching him.
Candles at *La Virgen*'s feet like flaming guards
swing their silvery sabers
in front of his brown eyes, warm intimate creatures
that ask forgiveness from the mysterious marble.

It's December and he has a gray coat on.
He makes the sign of the cross
and slowly rises. The altar behind him:
thorn-studded slits of flame in blue and red candle jars
spring and twist like a net
wrestling with a wild animal it's caught . . .

Outside again, before sunset,
the church bells
bellow through the wild grasses,
the notes trample across the distant fields
like great horses that drag boulders.
They breathe powerfully from steel nostrils;
and behind them great
clouds of sunlight explode
then simmer into evening.

Four

As if, when I was born, the doctor gave the blanket
I was swaddled in to a police hound to sniff,
and while judicial clerks tabulated future statistics
for how many policemen would have to be hired,
                I slept in a dream of lavender folds
                in my crib,
                my flesh over my bones
                like those long floor-to-ceiling curtains
                in palaces,
                I dreamed another world beyond me,
                of horses and women and food,
                of fields and dancing and songs,
unknowing that when I was carried from the hospital
in my blanket,
a police dog snarled at my passing,
a new set of handcuffs was being made,
and in the distance a new prison was being built.

At an early age
A heavy Bible was placed in my hand,
You got to get down and work hard, they told me.
You can't be talking back.
Whatever you do, watch out not to get in trouble,
     'cause they'll be looking for you,
       expecting you to get in trouble, they said.

Trouble was the furthest thing from my mind
when I knelt in a church
or climbed the rickety choir loft stairs to sing,

o love was me, o happy was I, young child
hypnotized by the stained-glass window
eye of God
circled above the altar back wall
dawn effused and made glow with blue robes
angels and doves
as I sang Latin hymns,
opening my mouth as wide and wholesome as a frog
on a pond in the full-moon summer night,
while shadows of pigeons flurried on the edge of the stained-
glass window—
Lord, I didn't see no blood of mine spilling on the dirt,
Lord, that others thought I was bad
had predestined my fate
to fall early,
struck later in life
from the blind side
by one clean sweeping stroke of law
I couldn't foresee
because I was too blinded by the blaze of beauty around me,
too in love with an old man's walk and cane
to even think he might curse a mean fate on me,
too in love with vigorous icy air of dark dawn
to think others might be plotting my future
at the hands of jailers.

But violence followed me.
On a cold November dusk, boys' brown arms cold and numb,
noses sniffling, dust in our hair, smudged cheeks,
while bats flitted like black gloves
from leafless trees, and on the distant freeway semis
gutted the air with growls,
while all the boys on the playground were blending
into the shades
of evening,
I turned from the sandbox,

my nose running mucus, my fingers dark crickets
in the sand, I turned and saw

> a big Indian boy by the fence,
> from his hand a thick coil of chain
>> slurped
> onto the ground, whiplike,
> and across from him a blond boy
> with blue eyes, in a torn T-shirt
> in midwinter, both approached
> warily as tigers on my brother,
> backing him off into the fence,

and then by an elm tree I saw a huge brown stone
on the ground,
and I dashed for the rock, picked it up, ran at the white boy
who had hit my brother and lunged at him with the rock,
hitting him on the head,

> falling back on the ground with him,
> at five years old, war-blood on my hands,

my heart screaming

> as if it had been bitten and ripped
> to shreds by bats

and since then
violence had always followed me—
in trees, down sidewalks, crouched in bushes, behind houses,
it leaps on me as I stand to confront
other bullies beating a thousand other brothers and sisters.

Five

Portate bien,
behave yourself, you always said to me.
I behaved myself
when others were warm in winter
and I stood out in the cold.

I behaved myself when others had full plates
and I stared at them hungrily,
never speaking out of turn,
existing in a shell of good white behavior
with my heart a wet-feathered
bird growing but never able to crack out of the shell.
Behaving like a good boy,
my behavior shattered
by outsiders who came
to my village one day
insulting my grandpa because he couldn't speak
     English
     English—
the invader's sword
the oppressor's language—
that hurled me into profound despair
that day Grandpa and I walked into the farm office
for a loan and this man didn't give my grandpa
an application because he was stupid, he said,
because he was ignorant and inferior,
and that moment
cut me in two torturous pieces
screaming my grandpa was a lovely man
that this government farm office clerk was a rude beast—
  and I saw my grandpa's eyes go dark
  with wound-hurts, regret, remorse
  that his grandchild would witness
 him humiliated
and the apricot tree in his soul
was buried
    was cut down
    using English language as an ax,
    and he hung from that dead tree
    like a noosed-up Mexican
    racist vigilante strung up ten years earlier
    for no other reason than that he was different,
    than that they didn't understand

                    his sacred soul, his loving heart,
                    his prayers and his songs,
Your words, *Portate bien,*
resonate in me,
and I obey in my integrity, my kindness, my courage,
as I am born again in the suffering of my people,
in our freedom, our beauty, our dual-faced,
dual-cultured, two-songed soul
and two-hearted
        ancient culture,
        me porto bien, Grandpa,
                    your memory
                    leafing my heart
                    like the sweetly fragrant sage.

But the scene of my grandpa in that room,
what came out of his soul
        and what soared from his veins,
        tidal-waving in my heart,
        helped make me into a poet
singing a song that endures and feeds
to make my fledgling heart
an eagle,
that makes my heavy fingers
strum a lover's heart and
create happiness in her sadness,
that makes the very ground in the prairie
soil to plant and feed the vision of so many of us
who just want to dance and love and fly
that makes us loyal to our hearts
and true to our souls!

It's the scene
that has never left me—
        through all the sadness
                    the terrors
                    the sweet momentary joys

that have blossomed in me,
  broken me, shattered my innocence,
  I've
never forgotten the room that day,
the way the light hazily filtered in the windows,
the strong dignified presence of my grandfather
in his sheepskin coat and field work boots,
      that scene,
      the way the boards creaked under his work boots,
haunted me
    when my children were born at home
    and my hands brought them into this world,
    that scene was in my hands,
it echoed in my dreams, drummed in my blood,
cried in my silent heart,
was with me through hours of my life,
      that man behind the counter,
    his important government papers rattling in the breeze,
    disdainful look on his face,
    that scene, the door, the child I was,
my grandpa's hand on the doorknob, his eyes on me like a voice
    in the wind
    forgiving and hurtful and loving,
    to this moment—
      his eyes following me
      where I swirl in a maddened dance
      to free it from my bones,
    like a broken-winged sparrow yearning for spring
      fields,
    let the scene go, having healed it in my soul,
    having nurtured it in my heart, I sing its flight, out, go,
fly sweet bird!

But the scene that dusty day
    with the drought-baked clay in my pants cuffs,
    the sheep starving for feed
    and my grandfather's hopes up

that the farm-aid man
would help us as he had other farmers—

that scene framed in my mind, ten years old
and having prayed at mass that morning,
begging God not to let our sheep die,
to perform a miracle for us
with a little help from the farm-aid man,
    I knew entering that door,
        seeing gringos come out smiling with signed
            papers to buy feed,
                that we too were going to survive the
                    drought;

the scene with its wooden floor,
my shoes scraping sand grains that had blown in,
the hot sun warming my face,
        and me standing in a room later
        by myself,
after the farm-aid man turned us down
and I knew our sheep were going to die,
knew Grandfather's heart was going to die,
that moment
      opened a wound in my heart
      and in the wound the scene replays itself
      a hundred times,
      the grief, the hurt, the confusion
      that day changed my life forever,
made me a man, made me understand
that because Grandfather couldn't speak
English,
        his heart died that day,
        and when I turned and walked out the door
        onto Main Street again,
            squinting my eyes at the whirling dust,
            the world was never the same
            because it was the first time

I had ever witnessed racism,
how it killed people's dreams, and during all of it
my grandfather said, *Portate bien, mijo,*
behave yourself, my son, *Portate bien.*

Six

An education
learned by laughing
when a world raises its fist angrily,
squeezing life out of you,
    learned to accept dark cells
    like a businessman buys new shirts,
    and heartbreaks like a banker's tally sheet
    adding up the golden coins
    making me a rich man.

Learned by seeing beautiful women
destroyed by a beautiful word,
seeing men coping with hate
come out dirty and drowned,
and I've come out dirty and half drowned,
belly-up, emptied eye,
staring bleakly into a blank future.

I've seen more of myself in sadness, and lost myself
happily in other people's arms, and willingly
I've set no pace nor goal,
and the longer I stay in one place, the more I see,
my eyes
a woman's womb
never knowing what child I shall bear and bring forth
in seeing what I see, nourishing it with hope and faith,
or will the scar be my birthmark into this world,

for scars have been my hidden face
and soul-strength for a long time now.

My trade is living, learning, sharing meals with friends,
        is asking how I will make it tomorrow,
        is enjoying my friend's smile,
        is making the world a classroom and books his eyes
        and the teacher's voice the dawn.

Seven

Yellow school buses halt at small groups
of waiting mothers,
rebozos around their shoulders,
like their Indio ancestors
huddled around a fire at night.
The kids scamper off
like young buffaloes nudging
their mothers' hands to play,
but then they finally dash off.

If I were a teacher
I would roam them along
the Rio Grande; teach them silence,
to listen to the air
brushing sunlight on leaves,
the soft stroking of wind quills
on leaves, sisst-sist-sist,
slowly drawing across the leaf, leaving
thin streaks of yellow, then turning them red and gold—

they would understand that
the poem
is given away—

that golden leaves fall to earth,
to the black, warm steaming earth,
where the hands of roots
weave our gifts again into the whole picture
called life.

I would teach them to fight for solitude,
stand their ground like mountain rams—
do not let the city's nightlife
lure them away—demand, shivering
uncertainty in blood, demand solitude.

I would teach them to look—
face the tree and study the bark,
see how the grooves foretell
our lives, how rough-edged it is,
how it holds up the tree, encircling the soft, moist
bark inside. How the tree counts its years
in circles, completing its sorrow each autumn,
enduring its loss of innocence each winter,
turning to meet the circle it drew
with new leaves, offerings of leaves
quivering under the sun god.

I would teach them to walk on the earth
as humans: to regard the cities as they do
their log-cabin toys—shelved
after play hour, as they resume their lives
in the sunlight, under the moon, among the people.

Eight

I sensed angels in the Stix barrio,
creaking Victorian porch boards

as they peeked in windows
misting them with star breath.
I saw them walk children to school
each morning.
Angels in Sanjo
    gathered in the park
    behind the community center,
    where they sat on picnic benches
        cleaning their wings and sharing a cigarette.
Over in Barelas
    angels formed a procession
    and sang in unison
    under the shady elm-lined trees
    "*La Bamba*" and other tunes.

Perhaps the ones I enjoyed the most
    were the older angels roaming the crop fields
    in the South Valley,
    veterano angels, collecting light from corn kernels,
    the air shaded from the green sheen of the chile pepper,
        squash-pecking crows
        leaving gifts of black feathers
        the angels twirled
                in their fingers
                igniting noon
                whose warm light droused me
                    into dream siestas.

Those angels in Alameda barrio,
young brown-skinned black-haired
and muscled,
    laughed under the broad-chested cottonwoods
    flaunting aerial skills
    in acrobatic flights
        comet wings
        burning across the air.

                        *   *   *

Over in Southside barrio
these angels could cook like you wouldn't believe—
they recited poetry while wrapping steaming tamales,
citing scripture as they roasted and peeled chile,
outdoors barbecuing lamb,
sometimes children would turn,
overhearing a psalm
    whistled on the air,
        they'd run thinking
        it was *la llorona*, the invisible witch.

Resonant chords and melodies
    flowed across Martineztown rooftops,
    mesmerizing old men with hairy ears
    playing checkers in front yards
    adjusting their hat brims from sunlight
    to doze to an angel's accordion song.

I saw angels everywhere,
    not as lapel pins or emblems or statues
    but accompanying me downtown
    I'd witness them
        by the old train station blessing rag-bundled hoboes,
        by Rex's snooker hall carrying drunks home,
        by the KIMO Theatre holding a child back
            from running into the street.

And in my life, when asked how I made it,
    I replied that I had a lot of angels
        helping me.

Nine

How we love our barrio
because the cherry tree's pink blossoms
were once tablecloths for our hearts,
where every hour was a pipe organ
trailing us with music
while stones yawned like puppies
licking at our small hands with splinters in them,
still smelling of buttered tortillas,
frijoles, *chile verde y arroz.*
            The breeze
            in the choir loft of trees
            is an altar boy
            gustily singing praise to Christ,
sunlight
            as it curls shyly like flowers
            in the old woman's graying hair
            as she hangs her husband's work jeans
            on the backyard line.
No matter that we become successful,
move to the suburbs and shop at malls,
our hearts simmer with sweet incense
of memories
when we remember
sun in the dirt yards
like cave dwellers' fire
            our bones the rubbing sticks
sparking flame to our adventurous sightings
in our endless reveries of roaming
alleys, field paths,

Rio Grande shores,
through the bosque and along the ditches,
        we followed the light
           the way we followed the conductor's tail of a stray dog,
           flickering off a rooster's fiery feathers,
           and laughed at the kettledrum shaking of a horse's head,
           or heard the flamed flicker of a coyote's yelp at night
                and the woosh't crackling
           of an old man burning brittle tumbleweeds
           as we heard the light humming an ancient
           symphony that celebrated our beings.
But more than that,
we've never forgotten the voices of the land,
the texture of lives lived that glowed each dawn
like a healing balm we'd later use
on our sore hearts
when we tried to be who we dreamed we could be—
           somehow the basketball points
           we scored were never enough
           to bring us happiness,
           nor did the work of our hands
           ever create the joy
           a simple sparrow did beyond our window;
somehow the bigger paychecks
didn't fulfill our hunger for the innocence
we dizzied ourselves in, the whirling hoops of lights
that circled us with moon rings
           in a time when our young hearts
           were the source of blinding radiance
           and we were dreams and our dreams were us
           and dusty winding roads we skipped and hopped every day
                echoed in grumbling dust clouds
           a grandfatherly love for us.
As we grew older
we couldn't touch the light again,
nor reinvent it from drugs, alcohol and religion,
nor from women we've loved or fistfights,

it stayed when we married and had children
and moved our families into better neighborhoods,
the light, along with the sun-scorched elm trees,
stayed, bidding us good-bye one day
as we drove our nice cars away,
the trees like distracted children playing barefoot in puddles
waved to us,
and the stray dogs sniffed at toads,
goats tolled their neck bells,
cows groaned and horses neighed,
each a ray of light
scraping like sharp knife blades
at our humble hearts,
leaving the apple peelings of our days
to compost back into the ground we loved so
much.
Our heaven was made of apple peelings,
beautiful Chicana woman cleaning beans on the table and
laughing loud,
the fervid scent of sage and piñon wood in the stove,
the subtle flirting of curtains billowing
from a draft on a warm summer afternoon,
a single voice of a mother calling her children,
her voice on the breeze
like a small angel carrying love.
The tattooed *vato locos,*
wandering in smoke and fog and mist,
with a brother in prison and another in college,
had sacred hearts and died young
falling asleep on couches
their cigarettes burning the cotton and killing them
because there was no light.
The barrio gave all of us
hearts that are sundials
imprinted with the sun's beam of love,
making moments crystalline glitterings

dripping all around us, so when we ran into Mama's kitchen
out of breath and fragrant with field-play,
bright lights scattered from our mouths and eyes and fingers and heels,

     The bright city lights never shone as intimate
     as the Rio Grande's water surface at dusk,
     burning water
     and blackbirds like blown ashes
     gliding over the air.
Never did the slick city streets
offer us vivid starlight
as the crusty dirt clods we crushed in our hands
to discover roly-polies—

we ran to catch dust devils
     spreading our arms wide in it,
     we spun like angels in the yard,
     spinning, spinning the sparkling thread of our souls
     into all life, weaving our souls and hearts
     into weeds and roses and people,
     playfully waving sticks like wands
          as black and red ants carried our sorrow away
          grain by grain to a smooth dune
          where moonlight danced the polka
          like Grandma and Grandpa in the kitchen,
          turning her, lifting her,
          raising her up
          like bread rising in the oven,
          filling the air
          with a wonderful savoring hunger for a life
          glowing with lights
          that made even the raindrops dangle from leaves and
               fence wires
               like musical notes, composed
               for a song celebrating the heart.

                         *   *   *

Haunted by the light of those days and the land,
driving back from the grocery store
or paying bills or on an errand
tired and sad,
in the night my car goes down a road,
swishing through wet streets,
when suddenly the green grass and road weeds
scatter their dewdroplets of light
    across the windshield
      each carrying a shivering moon
        that represents all the hearts
        ever born
        and it makes me weep
        for having had what I keep searching for
        in all I do.

Ten

Intimate moments on this night,
the young, beautiful woman in her green trench coat and head scarf,
cheeks chilled from the winter wind,
waits beside the Russian olive tree
to cross the busy street,
remembers the orchard
when she and her now-diseased father picked apples
and she licked the dew
and felt herself sparkle
with light words, light laughter, light gestures
radiating from her ten-year-old limbs.

The young man with his walking cane,
in his puffy down coat
briskly climbing up the hill with his dog

in his upper-class neighborhood,
pauses to catch his breath and blow his nose,
recalls a Christmas thirty-eight years ago
when his infant brother caught cold
and his lungs collapsed and he died,
how each Christmas after that, he'd taken these long walks
to speak in his heart with his absent brother.

The young Marine free of boot camp
driving to Gallup
faster than the speed limit,
anxious to get home to his mother's embrace
and cooking, to wrestle with his little brother
and pump off a hundred push-ups proudly,
doesn't know
that in one year his mother will receive a letter
from a war-wasted country that says he's dead.

The woman returning from New York
to visit her family in the South Valley
at Christmas, aglow with success and wealth,
sees how her childhood bedroom still has her dolls
propped on her pink-frilled bed pillow,
and her father in his rocking chair by the fireplace,
silent since his stroke, stares at the flames
and weeps as he sees her much younger,
riding his shoulder in the alfalfa fields,
her yelling,
I can almost touch the stars Papa, higher Papa.

The Vietnam vet remembers how his buddy
took pills and drank a bottle of tequila
and never woke up,
and how in Sacra, his friend Daniel's studio burned down,
thirty-five years of painting, sculptures, weavings,
songs, and how Daniel dances out his grief

in an Azteca dance with his children and wife,
making his loss a dance his children will dance
at festivals and celebrations,
how his burning studio will be strummed, drummed and sung
in dances.

My own intimate moments are of those men I've known
men who can't express themselves
        but don't hesitate to dive from bridges
                to save a drowning child or woman
                        and yet can't speak a word
                                on behalf of themselves.
Men who work day and night
        accustom themselves to four hours' sleep a night
                for years
                        without complaint
                                and can't utter a feeling.
Who sacrifice their youth and strength and good looks
                happily to ensure their family
                has a roof, food, warm beds and running cars.
                Their love is quiet
like the penny on the street no one picks up,
they love opera and baseball games on the radio,
and the best of their dreams are as simple
as the black-and-white TV
        their parents first bought,
                and their love is deep as the worn
                hoe handle
                glossed with a man's hands gripping it
                        fifty years,
their courage is a fireplace flame at night
still flickering in the morning when the kids wake up.

Men who've never been to a theater play,
who have a sense of what poetry is
                reciting verses from Paul Bunyan,

backward boys
     who'd rather be up to their shoulders
          in broken-down farm tractors
          oil pans and gunnysacks,
who never wept into the phone asking their parents
          for money to make a down payment
          or cosign on a car,
who never blamed their father or mother for their shortcomings
or had a need to display rings, necklaces, bracelets
but have worn the same old burnished watchband and watch,
and when visiting university campuses with their kids
appreciated the cut of hedges
and masonry on the old redbrick buildings,
who feel more comfortable listening
to Catahoula hounds crooning
than romantic songs on the radio,
who aren't religious but kneel in church now and then
     to thank God for their blessings,
who don't need yakking politicians
     to decide what's wrong and right,
          and hold a child in their hands
          gentle as a prairie wind
          grazes limber and lovely hill grass,
who enjoy a simple walk after supper
     appraising the sky for rain or noting the lay
     and condition of a neighbor's field,
who wouldn't hesitate to give apples or pumpkins to children
cavorting in the orchard or crop,
     but who never could speak their feelings
          when asked
          remained quiet and looked down
               at the earth
               what might be said
                    when actions speak so loud
for those who can't sing the thunder out of their veins.

Eleven

Graffiti on walls. Large tablets of stone Moses Sedillo
scribbles on about freedom. Our Berlin walls
our Juarez border. Agents in helicopters, others
in green jeeps, insomniacs with yellow faces lit
by monitor screens, check buses, cars, trucks and pedestrians—

and Moses Sedillo scribbles on about freedom.

In October the freedom of leaves changing colors, burying
        themselves in the
ground. Small golden coffins floating down the ditches.
        And then the
wiry, haggard branches become old men tottering behind
        the coffins,
fallen in the dirt road, leaning against fences. Moses
        throws himself
on the park grass and smells the green grass, the black earth, the
fine, thin coldness of the atmosphere.

He scribbles about freedom on walls.
No one knows what he means. The cops label him a vandal.
        The upper-middle-
class folks from the Heights are filled with fear, and the people
        in Santa Fe are angry
when they see his black letters on white adobe walls. Moses gives a
nondescript shrug of indifference and walks about the
        mountains and arroyos,
in the midst of aspens, thinking of beauty.

                    *   *   *

But Viviano from Nicaragua knows what Moses is saying.
Karina from El Salvador reads the words to her children after she buys
                              tortillas from the store.
Perfecto Flores, el viejo del barrio who goes to visit his
                    brothers every month in Durango, understands
                    the graffiti.

When the wall is painted over, the words push through the paint
    like prisoners' hands
                          through prison bars
                          at strangers passing on the streets.

Twelve

Fingers—
I won't go into all the work they've done,
          more interested
    how they ignore
    manners when scratching or picking.
          Seeing women
standing below in dark rain on an evening winter night
on the street signaling their lovers in jail
signing messages of love and grief
                          fondling and caressing the air,
          patting their dog-scruff hearts,
    gripping the steering wheel of grief
          or the prisoners above signing back
          codes that send the women off on missions
          to collect drugs or send messages to friends.
                    A hand sign with crimped and bent fingers
          studded with cheap rings
          has only one need in life—to communicate—
                    isn't that the essential reason we do what we do,
          to communicate to another human being?

To communicate
how much we love, how much we desire to be touched,
to be loved and love someone,
    the spinster's fingers grow thin
    like witnesses to a crime, and hold secrets to themselves,
    the poet's fingers singe the air
    like loose electrical wires whipping around in a storm—
        but it is the fingers of those women on the streets
        that keep true to what fingers
        were meant to do—
                communicating
                    messages of loyalty,
                    the fingers say

We haven't forgotten you,
yes, I will come to visit you on Friday,
no, your mother has to work
    changing sheets at the hospital,
your little brother was arrested last night,
    of course I'll dream of you,
    I'll think of you
    with every spoon of chile and bite of tortilla
    I'll see you in the window
  when the wind is blowing,
    I'll ask God to bless you and I'll wait, my love,
    I'll wait, my love, forever.

✳   ✳   ✳

Sunday service on the street,
he signs up to his woman behind bars
how her mother combed her daughter's tangled hair
before church, how her uncles
drank too much wine and played violin and accordion
and woke up the whole barrio,
bringing widows in their nightgowns out on porches
to reminisce about days before their husbands abandoned them.

✻   ✻   ✻

She signs him back
all night guards' footsteps kept her awake,
the woman next to her breathes too loud in her sleep.

While motorists go by in a hurry for Christmas shopping
and pedestrians glance meanly at him,
they never guess he is signing her
promises to keep their love strong,
vows to wait for her, praying for God to bless them.
More than that
is what he left unsaid
when her time was up and another woman
stood by the bars signing her man—
left unsaid
his loneliness felt like a stone dwelling,
his temporary refuge from the world of consumers
because he didn't have money for any presents,
except to create his space on the street corner
in the chaos and craze of this holiday season,
but when he signed freedom—
flickering and twisting his fingers
fighting upstream toward
their original spawning waters of her heart
that they must hold on to each other,
raging back toward what they feel
where they belong,
with each other, holding hands
in the black mothering evening waters
she understood.
But left unsaid is without her,
in the midst of his loneliness,
each dawn, his hope and dreams come forth,
blood drops shivering on dagger blades.

*   *   *

You sign checks
she signs love

you signal for waiters
        she signals warnings to dealers
                you raise your hands to heaven
                she raises hers to block blows
                        you use yours to embrace
                        hers are to push away
yours to turn book pages
hers to count end-of-the-day earnings
                to gas up, grub down a burger
                and hit the streets again,
                        so she'll take it to you
                        because there's a war going on,
                        in the streets, in jails, everywhere
                                beyond her barrio
                        is where the enemies live—
Angry?
Pissed off?
Hating?
Lonely?
Vengeful?
Hurt?
Unloved?
Despised?
Ostracized?
                        Damn right,
                        so clear off the streets when the sun goes down
                        because darkness has always been hers,
it's where she's lived all her life
                        and she can see in the dark,
                        cry in the dark,
                        eat and love and hurt in the dark,
                it's hers and it's all we gave her,
                so when she catches us there in it,
she doesn't give a shit who we are, what color we are,
                she'll bring it to us,
make us feel a little of the darkness
                she's felt and lived in all her life.

Be sentimental about rehabilitating her,
              flatter ourselves by thinking
                      we can change her,
             send all our goodwill counselors
             and face-polished probation officers,
but she ain't changing shit because it's all based on a lie,
             a muthafucking lie,
             telling her she's supposed to be poor,
             that justice is for the rich and privileged,
she knows when you take away every chance and opportunity
before she's even born,
             if we build a prison cell for her to live in
             predicting she'll be a criminal,
             if we take away
her essential need to communicate, the tiniest chance she has
to scrape crumbs of dignity off the table,
if we devise ways to make her feel inferior,
to make her feel different than others more acceptable,
if we call her a spic and nigger and white trash
and expect her to be our house servant,
             our fort-Indian or Mexican gardener—
             Muthafucka, she screams,
             I need to communicate
             to another human being!
I got to
      in some way
            feel that I'm a human being
                 and I do so with my hand flashing
                 signs on the street corner
                 like a woman lost at sea
                 flagging down a ship to save me
but the only ones who stop are cops to beat me up
so don't you understand that someday
I'll come knocking at your door
and what sins you ignored
your sons and daughters and grandchildren

are gonna pay for,
don't you understand
you got to pay the bill
in the form of blood on a blade
'cause you never wanted to communicate—
I got so many things I want to know
and am willing to try
but the only time you ask questions,
the only time you give a damn
is when I'm in front of a judge asking me how I plead
or cops asking me what I'm doing
or enemies challenging me
or teachers accusing me
    or counselors profiling me as a bad girl
    or priests condemning me as a sinner going to hell
    or citizens mob-hanging curses at me
        how it's my fault their lives
        don't line up to their bank-book fantasies,
but no one's ever asked
    How you doing?
    Can we talk, you want to come over to my house,
    meet my family,
        let's play ball tomorrow,
        you hungry I'll fix something to eat,
        come over when you want to talk,
        let me know if you need anything,
here's a little food money,
maybe I can help you with a job,
        sure I'll go to the judge and talk
        on your behalf,
        sure you can come over when you got nowhere
            else to go,
instead it's all "she ain't nothing but a criminal
should be locked up
should be put in a cell forever"
        I want to communicate,
        talk to someone about who I am,

what dreams I have,
tell you that I've been there
that I know who you are
did I tell you?
But you won't let me communicate that,
you just want me off the face of the earth,
never to have been born,
never to have had a name,
no songs, culture, parents, siblings . . .

Thirteen

Her hands are earth swans
surrendering only to love,
cupping her right hand,
her fingers turned down smoothly
into a graceful neck,
and pointing up, her left middle finger
in the pad of her palm,
her index and thumb in a circle
both together
a swan that swims untouched
through streams of police bullets,
lakes of drugs and hypodermic needles,
nestling her infant under her wings
of black hair and sumptuous breasts,
unscathed by drive-bys, by stab wounds,
by violent fights with her boyfriend,
she glides each dawn like a mother's hands
folding cloth diapers and smoothing out
little-boy shirts and pants,
warm and clean and soft,
            her hands
            her beautiful hands.

*   *   *

So many times her wings have opened
to cover her face to absorb tears
glistening as if from heaven down upon her feathery hands,
so many times they've been drenched
in blood, angrily fluttering from racists and snobbery bigots,
so many times she's shaken her winged hands
at people who don't like the way she looks—
yet she's surrendered her hands to her lovers,
given them to making tortillas and beans and chile,
offered them in prayer to God
like cathedral doves fluttering around the bell tower
at sunrise, joining the white doves
on stained-glass windows, to merge them with angel wings.

Instead of leaving her handprints on rocks
or a slap imprint on a cheek,
her palms are prints in hearts
that resemble solitary undiscovered beaches
where the tides are her whispered kissings.
Hers are not the hands that punish,
nor are they aristocratic hands and fingers
whose touch is chilled porcelain,
they're hands that heal wounds, strip corn husks,
brush on blood-red nail polish and scarlet lipstick,
the kind of hands that appear in martyrs' dreams
and the kind convicts and beggars reach for
to touch and relieve their despair—
              she brings her hands to the world
              with schoolgirl innocence,
              shows the world
how they feel and the wondrous things they can do
to bring love to loveless ones,
to soothe the heartache in drunks,
to ease the grim guillotine swinging across each night
for addicts as they search for a fix—
              to know her,

understand her fingers and hands,
       touch them as you might touch
       a child's sleeping face—
       Come feel my hands
       and remember when you were a teenager
       dreaming of love
       riding in a battered '72 Galaxy
       beneath a long row of cool cottonwoods,
       remember how you lost your beloved
       first love,
       feel how my hands lift your sorrow
       and allow yourself to fly in the green, sun-shimmering
          leaves
          losing yourself in the blue sky,
            in blue sky . . .

Fourteen

Last night she dreamed her fingers
were crucifixes
that dangled from her wrists,
       rusty nails of trust
and betrayal
hammered into the small bones.
Nonetheless, each finger is a ballerina
moving to its own grief and joy,
   silently,
complaints and joy
outrage and hurt
   move across the air in forms
learned from cooking and cleaning,
bathed in tears, in touching her lover's
lips, caressing his flesh with the heart-
beat just beneath

like a song that keeps coming
after friends have gone and she finds
herself unemployed—dreaming,
        her fingers are good at dreaming,
and she stands each morning beneath the jail windows
signaling dreams to her love behind the bars,
signaling the old song
that her fingers will hold his love,
remember his love, prepare for his love,
        dreams intact,
        at the end of the day
when everything is quiet, distant gunshots in the barrio
and ghetto crack the air with spite
and murderous hisses,
        she stares at her fingers on the table
and with a girlfriend, paints them red,
paints them in brilliant flakes
        soft pink and hot orange,
        preparing the small dancers to go out into the night
to talk with her love again,
standing at the street corner, signing
her lover's street-warrior code behind enemy lines.

She is one of those who brings food to the soldiers
fighting cops and going to prison,
one of those who will never give in,
they'd have to cut her fingers off one by one,
hang them like dried flowers upside down from a cord
in the wind and sun, withering
witnesses to the injustice and passion of each day's struggle
just to have someone to love and receive love from,
        not till that day
will the ballerinas quit dancing beneath the sun and moon.

Fifteen

His brother Pablo's photograph
    on his *jefita's* mantel
    salutes him every night
        he comes in late
        wearing his sag and bags,
        sometimes high,
        stoned on sweet bud,
he feels his brother's eyes scolding him
        from his serious Marine face
        but that salute pisses him off
        because his brother died
in a war run by political crooks who never gave a damn
about Chicanos or Chicanas.
        He'd much rather have seen him flashing a
        barrio sign
        in defiance of the military,
outlaw on the run, but his *jefito* says to die for the Marines
is an honor. His brother would be sleeping in the room next to his
if he were alive, and in his own honorable way of loving him
he makes his brother's Marine salute part of his barrio
        sign—
too,
      that school crossing guard holding up his white-gloved
hand for him to stop and let parents and kids go by—
he's turned his uplifted hand
        into part of his barrio hand signs
        signaling homeboys to stop
        what they're doing, *Ay viene la joda,*
           Truchas!

Ojo Aguila!
Cuidao!
His index finger taps his left eye and they know
to watch out;
     he's even picked up signs from politicians
     caught scamming, and he watches how they drop one hand
     innocently and raise the other explaining
their saintliness,
Nixon throwing his peace sign,
the savings-and-loan hustle where that guy
carried his Bible in court (good move),
Milken who made millions from junk-bond rip-offs
on Wall Street,
with a stash of sixty million in the bank
shaking the judge's hand after being sentenced
to six months' country club time—
     he took Milken's slick shake and changed it
to his money shake—
a straight four-fingers-out slide,
slipping either money or a dime-paper
of coke into a customer's palm.
     Even Clinton uses a pointed finger
     to describe his innocence,
pointing his pinkie up and moving it sideways
to say he didn't do it, he didn't do it,
     but the most important sign of all that he's learned
     is when law-abiding citizens
     take the stand and raise their hand
     vowing to tell the truth and nothing but the truth,
he's turned that sign when he raises his hand like that
     to mean all bullshit,
     all bullshit.
The signs that mean truth, that he works hard at forming
     contorting his fingers,
     he gets from *viejas del barrio*
     with arthritic hands,
     from hands swollen from decades of hard work,

from hands of *viejos* who have hoed and picked
in fields all their lives—
those are the signs that are really hard to mimic
because they're so real.
His signaling started when he was a child:
he'd darken his room
all except for his lamp and make his hands
a silhouette bird flying on the wall
touch his thumbs together and make his fingers waver
like flying wings on the wall.
          That sign became his
                    We're outta here
                    to homegirls across the park,
and then you know how *la placa* (cops), when they arrest you,
put out your hands, palms up in front of you,
so they can handcuff you?
          Well, he invented a sign
where your elbows touch just above your belly button
and your arms go up in a V,
          but instead of putting your hands together
like being handcuffed,
          you open the V wide at your hands to symbolize *Let's go!*
               You're free!
Geese flying in V formation—
but you want to know what's the most powerful sign of all,
the one that means he has heart and pride
and he'll stand up
for his *Indigena Raza,* fight to the death
against any intruder
trying to take his family apart
or harm his loved ones?
It's when he's got
his arm crooked so his fist is by his heart,
his fist raised a little,
denouncing all the lies and money-grubbers,
          watch out and don't get in his way
          when he has his fist raised like that

it means he's doing what he's doing from his heart,
it means don't mess with him,
it means he's there in that zone
where he loves all of who he is.

Sixteen

Cut-tongued sparrows
        watch for snakes
as they gather by gates,
under windows, bridges, arches
their nests pillaged
like coins bagged from slot machines
by casino profiteers.

The days repeat themselves
        babbling in dream speech their despair,
        reference fractured,
        the cut-tongued sparrows whirl
        beneath concrete branches,
        culture or history molted from them
        like feathers
                collected by healers
        in a world where ebbs and tides
        have no shores,
        where rap is piped through snub-nosed .45s,
        where schoolchildren set fire
        to schoolbook pages,
                and wedge-cut trees with lovers' initials,
                bark maps that grieve,
their primitive nomad sadness
        as they huddle on street corners
        opening their hands to sign—

                        *   *   *

Police-gunned
and exiled, unable to execute,
the composition of their lives
        a canvas spattered with
                their red-blood screams.

Their hands are bilingual sea spray,
      snap and sparkle
      tropical expressions on winter reefs,
      storm-slung split-tongued yeastings
      fermented from street bog-muck
      and PCP-laced beer-foaming forties
      in which they soar in lagoon reveries
      remembering
      absent fathers and mothers
      sentimental as dogs slavering
      at the wind
      sniffing and barking.

      Cut-tongued sparrows
            who migrate in gutters,
            dirt birds who bathe in soil,
            cockroach-eating birds,
      don't know where they come from,
      who they are, where they're going,
      scratch, peck, chirp violently
      of destruction, drugs and sex
            bantering bullshit,
            warm up against one another
                 in police lineups
            not telephone wires,
            criminalized in reed lands of cell bars,
whose high-tech lives
      are digitally read out via satellite sound waves,
      arrested, charged and jailed.

                    *   *   *

Yet munching on number-ones and number-twos
at Burger King for breakfast,
        they laugh about basketball
                and chicks, hanging tough
with their souls' eyes pecked out,
their hearts' tongues split in two,
        cold-cheeked in the dawn,
        whose parents kicked them out,
                raging stepfathers beating on them,
                their blood dads remarried with other families,
only the rising sun welcomes them each day
dressed in basketball T-shirts
                unlaced Jordan Nikes
                        braid belts, earrings
                                in pro-football jackets
                                headphones ripping a tune by Tupac
they laugh, talk smack, trash nine-to-fivers
        whacked-out bill-paying squares,
somehow
        they survive and keep their hope alive,
        somehow
                the cut-tongue sparrows
                keep singing and inventing and creating
                their lives.

Seventeen

At the Paint & Body Shop
the burrito lady arrives among the cut-tongued sparrows
and sells workers burritos
from an ice-cooler in her trunk.
Munching them with one hand,
the workers work, taping, primering

sanding and drilling holes
in the steel husks of autos.

I wait for them to finish screwing the side mirrors
and chrome trim on my '66 Chevy,
working at a nonchalant pace.
The boss cradles an infant, his plump wife follows him
from an empty paint bay into the office
and back into the paint bay,
the whole time he's goo-gooing da-daaing his baby
with intimate, cuddly sounds.

I step outside, studying the wrecked cars that crowd the weedy lot—
with bullet holes in the doors,
shattered windows, crushed fenders,
newer fiberglass cars by the crippled fence
choked with weeds.
        I think of the love songs these cars sounded
        when they once cruised Main Street
honking at the babes, babes honking at the boys,
now the ritual of our romance
is splintered evidence of our eagerness
toward a dream and our helplessness to catch it.
Above the busted iron bulks and frayed frenzied dash wires
a dead-bulb neon sign dangles on a broken chain,
lost in crisscrossed, clotted telephone wires, shivering slightly
            from highway tractor trailers
            scissoring and shearing the air
            on the nearby freeway.

Back in the office
wallboard plaster still drying,
untrimmed doorframe;
free countertop ink pens and shirt-pocket calendars
advertise religious conversions
along with the name of the shop.

                    *   *   *

A radio blasts oldies but goodies
as Chicanos and Indios labor side by side,
and watching them, I remember being one of them—
        in paint-smeared faded jeans,
        cut-off T-shirt, brawned forearms and biceps rippling
        with every stroke and swipe of sandpaper
        on the rough primer, smoothing it softer than a baby's behind.
        Laughing easily in bright sun, one of them
                    with flowers breaking through my stone heart
                    in those earthquake-youthful days.
My life was so vibrant and I reeled in optimism,
contemptuously dismissing rock stars and matinee idols
because we were the ones who had the life,
        tutoring flower children from 'Frisco in matters of love,
        skinny-dipping in mountain springs with New York dolls,
        partying with L.A. chicks
                who loved our Indio-Chicano culture
                and our dope, homemade brew and hot chili
        who made candles and incense in our adobe houses,
        climbed up on viga ladders to the roof
        high on peyote and mushrooms
                to watch the stars and moon.

Red ants trickle on the cracked sidewalk,
entering undisturbed through the open front door.
        Life was never about books,
        we looked to crows and hawks for messages,
        our Friday check was all the messiah we needed
                        to make life good
        and to ease our rock-and-roll booze-guzzling nights,
        our windowpane-acid days,
        to get us by our heartbreaks and breakups,
        our confusion, fear, despair and joy,
we had our work at the body shop
where we could tell our lies and share our woes,
        waking up unwashed and going straight to work,
that day between the car dismantled like shattered crockery

and Jimi Hendrix groaning out blues tunes, we'd decide to leave
for 'Frisco to hear the Grateful Dead or Denver
                              to hear Joplin at Bear Stadium—
Today those friends have kids who deal drugs
while going to night school,
and when I ask about their fathers, they say
so-and-so's in a wheelchair, another one got stabbed and has only
      one lung,
others tramp dusty railroad paths carrying worn-out dreams
infused with drugs and wine, on a tree stump or torn-up sofa
in the cool shade of a yard, they reminisce about the old days.
Wounded and wiser veterans of life lived,
having endured gangs, crime, violence, poverty, racism
but not gone silent,
instead
like jaguars scratching at cage floors
      your blunt clawings groove the concrete
      with your yearning for freedom—
I see so many of you on the roadside
in county-jail orange jumpsuits with numbers,
hoeing weeds and picking up trash,
and I also note how motorists
      give you righteous glances. Yes, brothers and sisters,
life is very unjust, but we roll with gods beating in our blood,
even hoeing weeds, we do it with class and style.

            I go back out,
studying the patchy weathered stucco
and utility lines that droop
      in tangled knots across the roof.
      I check out the backs of cars that haven't been touched
                              in years.
      Dusty, decrepit, decaying haven for the smashed and crushed
      casualties,
                  imagine their moments of death:
                  squealing rubber, whirling through space,
                        out of control,

```
                  prayers on lips,
                  screams,
            in the maddening lust and sensuous sexual
                  purrings
            of young, inciting love
on a summer evening,
under city lights,
sailing away from familiar lives, the violent
glass and iron mangling,
fire and smoke, the radio goes dead
then the moment of white silence, blood in the crusty gravel,
bodies in the weeds and whiskey-bottle fragments
like a gambler's hand folding a high flush of red heart cards.
```

Standing in the doorway
waiting for the workers to finish the trim,
I notice how significant their work is to them—
grimed, caked in pigments and dust, grease,
            bruises and cuts,
            they have that fulfilled, exhausted look
I used to have
      when I came home from work every night
      after gorging on burgers
      so tired I passed out in bed with my clothes on—

it was as if my pulse had a bumblebee in it
that departed each morning to collect pollen,
as if my heart were an old horny toad
savoring tasty insects and slumbering under stones,
      those grunt-sweating workdays
      were the purest of time.

I honor the callused hand that beads a necklace of humble memories
placed around a child's heart,
the dirty life that channels God through it like rainwater,
a child's birth in an old man's clear gazing eyes
that keeps him young—

suddenly, a rich guy drives his Porsche in
to get his dented door open,
and the workers grab their screwdrivers and pliers,
      gnawing at the locked door bolt,
      and they unlatch it, get it open,
and that's what they do, open doors,
they free things . . .

Eighteen

Yesterday, driving across the bridge with my friend,
the brilliant orange cottonwood leaves along the river
      made me think of love,
and the red plum tree
      next to the bus-stop bench
      of enduring resilience,
and the brown leaves in the gutter
my disappointments.
      I imagine a ghostly specter
      visiting my bedside
      and piling those brown leaves on my tiny heart.

That was when my friend asked me who or what
      did God give his unending blessings?
He expected me to say the innocent
      but I replied that God gives his blessings
      and miracles
         to what rots and is broken and is crumbling—
that which is decomposing, blessings in the rot,
in the dark matter that is breaking apart
like a fractured wall,
      bricks falling to the ground
         because life wants open fields,

not separation,
                everything integrating in one black mass
                of decreation and creation
        birthing and dying, in the wound is freedom,
        in the young crippled boy struggling to step
        up to the bus
the imperfect—
                walls everywhere, every business has barred windows,
walls, walls,
we admire the Mercedes driver with smoked tinted windows
his walls allow no intrusion,
but the hitchhiker's walls have come down:
the kid on the street corner
with purple locks
is saying look at my purple hair
it's my wall
but walls that fall are where life feasts on miracles
are where God lives and does the work
of true living
        opening fields up wide for us to run
and walk,
smashing down walls for strangers to finally see their neighbors,
freeing prisoners from their mansions, their prisons,
their racism, their fears, their ambitions, their greed,
        to celebrate
                life as they did when golden cottonwood leaves
piled high on their hearts.

At a coffee shop later
I thought of a dear friend who'd died
a drunk.
He'd come from a farm where only Spanish
was spoken, his music and laughter from those days
haunted him as he tried to assimilate
into an America that saw him as an enemy
because he was different.

His choices were to leave everything he loved
and everything he knew,
a culture robust with rituals, prayer and love,
to find solace in academia
to lose his identity, his soul, his heart
and embrace Taco Bell, be that scrawny runt of a dog
yapping *Yo quiero Taco Bell,*
but he couldn't,
        it repelled him, made him queasy
to think that one could sell out
to become a spineless, heartless Chihuahua
on the lap of a pinched-face middle-class housewife;
nor could he be the Chicano
against everything America stood for,
with a wealth of wisdom and heart
                courage and fierce determination to never sell out.
He knew the two were wrong,
                that he wanted a little of both
                but to be himself,
                to lounge in who he was
                        happily striving into the day
                        with a heart brimming full
                        of love for life.
The question of what kind of man would he be
sequestered him
                in limbo,
                to see a doctor or a *curandero,*
                to study books as the sole source of knowledge
                or dig deeper into his oral history
                        where he remembered
                        his grandpa could cure and heal
                        ailments in human or livestock.
                To stick with his customs or go forward
                into the bleak sterility of new cars and new houses
                in suburbs where no one ever talked to one
                        another.

And while he thought about the two,
                    the one who remedied injustice
by hiring a battalion of lawyers
or by killing the insulting enemy,
to be caged parrot or proud hawk,
to submit to being a lobotomized consumer
and mimic the sentiments of the boss
or wear his cultural clothes, speak his language,
        believe in the ancient gods
                and pray to his ancestors,
what to do?
And while he wrestled with this, he drank,
sat alone in bars and drained glass after glass,
sensing he had a bit of both in him,
        wondering how to keep intact
        the best of the two
        infuse the wonder for life
        with success in life,
how to feel comfortable in his brown Latino skin
how to feel proud of his culture
        or talk like gringos, focus only on money,
        dress in a manner befitting
                a well-oiled and slicked-greased American
immune from consciousness,
close his eyes, stop up his ears, hold his tongue,
restrain his trembling fists
when insolent racists smirked aloud at spics or wetbacks,
                and while he thought this out, he drank
                more and more whiskey
                until he started puking blood
and eventually had a brain hemorrhage
                and died.
There's a black round table with salt, pepper and Tabasco shakers
equally spaced apart so they're looking at one another.
Move any one of them around the table's edge
and it catches another, the one it despises.

The salt shaker finds itself behind the pepper,
        the Tabasco bottle finds it's now in front.
        The pepper shaker looks behind it
        and sees the salt shaker.
        Each keeps changing places, wondering what it's doing
        behind the one it thought it was in front of.
My friend couldn't change, couldn't sustain
        the gestation period,
                couldn't be the salt shaker one day,
                the pepper the next,
                        the Tabasco again,
                                and then all three,
                                        enriching his identity,
                                        growing
                                        from the raw resources
                                        added to the recipe
his parents made of him.
        He couldn't take the best of oral history
        and book readings
        the best of folk healing herbs
        and medical prescription,
        English and Spanish,
                Mexican culture
                        and American trends,
                                his heart asphyxiated
                                he turned purple
                                he tried to breathe
                                he fell to his knees
                                grabbing his throat
                                gasping for air
                                        and keeled over in the street.
And pedestrians stepped over him,
motorists drove by,
        a cop poked him with a billy club
                and walked on,
                others cursed him as a wino
                degenerate, anti-American

taking our jobs away, drug dealer
who should go back where he came from,
he came here for a free lunch,
he doesn't work,
he doesn't deserve to live.
Later in the day
I see the cottonwood tree's
golden, lime-green and reddish

                                        leaves

blend into one another
and realize what he wanted
                  was to take the changes of life
                  as the tree welcomes its leaves
                  and as the leaves change with seasons,
                  the magnificent tree is always there,
                        always there
                              in gray, green, gold,
                                    and sometimes just the
                                    rain-darkened boughs
racked and shaken by storms
will tell me more than I've ever learned in books
about what the heart should do.

Nineteen

Your father's life, Cindy, was a deep connection to earth.

When Father had to speak with her
he'd walk her out to the pasture
and tell her things in his heart,
      or under the cloud-reddening skies of dusk
      they'd walk the long dirt road to the main road,
      his words like eagles

she could pet, sitting on her shoulders,
        spreading black-edged white wings
        gliding over the ploughed fields
        swooping low over her heart
        plucking up what was bothering her
        to leave her lighthearted.

When you usually think of survival
how people survive in their village
how a village goes on living
        you don't realize it's done
        doing the small things—
        a man going out to the corrals
        built when he was a boy with his father,
        and you don't hear the song he hears
        shimmering in the furrows,
                you don't see God
                in the deer
that grazes with his cattle and sheep
in the field,
                or the scattering of blessings
                in flocks of crows
                whirling like a matador's black cape
                as he does—

if you're looking for peace,
if you want patience,
then go see those
folks who keep the small villages alive—
the old man crouching near the ground
and tossing pebbles out before him
is a prayer calling the gods to bless his day,
        his unbelievable warm and loving embraces
        are prayers for your good health.

                    ✿   ✿   ✿

Your father's life, Cindy, was a deep connection to earth.

I know that when these people die,
their last words are of how much they'll miss
their fields, the earth, the potato trucks
roaring into Main Street at midnight,
the hum of tractors baling at night,
they enjoyed each hole and rut in the dirt driveway,
jostling them like a loving mother
back and forth as they went to feed
the sheep each morning,
  each upturned dirt clod gave them
  self-esteem,
  each sprout of barley or wheat
    filled them with confidence,
    each flowering alfalfa leaf
    gave their hearts a banquet of joy.

And when the water's gladdening
baptized the soil,
  each plant and blade of grass
  humbly opened its petal-leaf hands
  to be anointed,
he was working in the heart of things,
felt himself consecrated with each step he took,
with each bead of sweat, each swing of the hoe,
each movement he made during the day he felt himself
in the presence of God,
  so if you come with your engineering plans,
  your business plans to develop,
  your factories spewing out toxic water,
  your urban developers,
    be aware you are killing God
    and his angels.
    Be aware
you are insulting generations of people
who have loved and worked the earth

generations before and generations after,
　　be aware you are clipping off the wings of angels,
cutting off God's hands,
　　brutalizing God's blessings,
　　disrespecting and torturing what was a source
of our humanity,
　　　　until dehumanized
　　　　we kill one another, we take drugs,
　　　　we insanely consume,
　　　　slaughtering
　　　　the very essence of what defines us
　　　　　　as human,
　　　　　　　　our connection
　　　　　　　　to God.

Your father's life, Cindy, was a deep connection to earth.

Remember, each ditch is an umbilical cord
and when you cut it
　　with paved roads,
　　city trucks and street-tarring crews,
　　when you trench out suburbs with backhoes
　　and lay plumbing pipes and wires
　　so each house has six bedrooms and washing machines,
　　four sinks and two showers and tubs,
every time we mindlessly turn on the faucet
to flush the toilet,
　　we are joining the well-lit neon modern age
　　and in equal measure darkening
　　　　the light in our hearts
　　until we become afraid to even look in our hearts,
　　afraid to face the terrible damage we've done
　　　　to our humanity,
　　blindly, we go forward, spiral into the abysm,
　　　　free-falling deeper into our dehumanization.

Your father's life, Cindy, was a deep connection to earth.

Twenty

And when they come, as they have,
       Grandma,
I seek strength in your humble memory.
As contrary and far-fetched as my metaphors
and images may seem
           to a woman
in the hot, dry prairie,
     when you walked I knew somewhere
in the world a great pianist was playing
to your steps,
     when you looked at beans, corn, squash,
a simple glass of water,
your gaze had a melody of a hundred choirs
singing in harmony, all in unison,
thanking the Great Creator for your many blessings.

O dear sweet ancient woman who never
uttered a word of pain on her behalf,
who was sometimes mean or cross with me,
who chased and shooed me from the house on wash day
or made me scrub my face with freezing-cold water,
your faults were cliff-edge fingerholds;
anyone brave enough to climb to the summit
would be rewarded with a sight only angels were given.
And I climbed there many times
     and as many you called me your angel.

Today, when I'm besieged by enemies from all sides,
when the easy way out haunts me,

when I would prefer to sit in a cantina and drink
with my friends,
when doing drugs with acquaintances to forget
the pain of living seems easier than to live with dignity,
when I promise to try harder,
when all these vows of conviction
weakly drain blood from my lips,
      I kiss your face again in my memory
and tell you to watch me, just watch—

I will not surrender to the worst part of myself
but be a man you can be proud of,
who has learned well from you, sweet Grandma.
And as they come, as they do, I wade out in the field,
briskly parting the tall weeds and ignoring the briars,
I move forward to meet them,
to show them that all their flags and hollering
and weapons mean nothing to me
when I have you in my heart.

When my heart brims with bubbling waterfalls cracking past
obstacles that have tried to prevent
my jaguar howling,
      my veins swell with fiery colt-jumps
in hefty alfalfa fields, and I must compose my songs
solemn as monks chanting in a medieval monastery,
dark stone and polished rock hallways echo my wailing
of sorrow and loneliness,
and at other times the maddened conga drums of my heart
are beaten by black hands, white hands, red hands, brown hands,
every race calling me to celebrate their humanity, their laughter, their
sadness,
and when all of this incredible emotion spews
from my whale's blowhole heart
as I rise from my deep blue sleep of everyday life,
I break water surface and Grandma, Grandma
how I think of you sitting

at the table cleaning pinto beans for supper that evening,
how you worried, how you smiled, how you grimaced
and how you went blind, your bones gnarled and crudely
twisted with age, and you gradually
rolled into a ball of ancient root-branch GOD-TREE
for someone like me to cling to during storms,
for someone like me to hide under during storms,
and I still do, Grandma—
                    and this poem
                    is my joy-song to you, sweet Grandma,
you vitalize my tongue to lick the minerals
of each day and become part earth as you were,
you prick my heels to encourage me to take the toughest path,
you whisper me to dream of love,
to believe in myself,
sitting there at the table in a small village on a summer afternoon,
cleaning pinto beans,
in every instance where I needed hope, love, help,
this image of you keeps me strong, keeps me moving on.

Book II

Meeting My Love,
True to My Heart
and Loyal to My Soul

One

I was here at sixteen,
when L.A. was still a place
where all my dreams would
        come true,
airborne seedlings
        greening my desert heart,
        and of course
            there would be a woman like you
            just for me,
to heal the pain and betrayal
of another
      who guzzled and licked me dry
      down to the last tongue-licking drop
      of my soul
      and left
         my feelings a stack of dirty dishes
         on the drain board,
            my banquet of dreams she'd gorged herself on,
            half-eaten hardening leftovers,
thrown away and left for black crows to glean in Albuquerque
    fields.
         I knew if my rusting '67 Bug
         made it over the nine-mile hill
      west of Burque,
      I'd make it all the way to L.A.
and I did—
hand-slapping Muddy Waters blues
on the steering wheel,
chugging to L.A., knowing when I got there
         the good life would roll in,

waves ebbing
                cool on my toes in the sand;
the good life
        fruit bowls laden with halos of oranges, apples,
                        tangerines, grapefruit,
        yard flowers smoldering radiant fragrance,
        lush, high grass
        tamped to a path by backpacking acid-head hippies
                        seeking Christ,
        or buzzed-out Brando-blooded blue-jeaned
                        bad boys on Harleys
                        lighting Lucky Strikes
                        with old-fashioned silver lighters.
The women would all have names
        that summoned to mind
        a Sonny Rollins saxophone tune
        their hips and hair scented candle flames
        in the breeze
        salty and moist as a lip-wet bamboo reed
        on the sax player's tongue
        curving up notes to the moon
        like tides pounding love against the pier pillars
shuddering the boards
with orgasms.

My dream endured,
        and it was when I finally met you, Lisana,
        after armies of brown faces seeking education and justice
                marched,
        after unending sidewalk cardboard cities swelled,
        after addicts begged for bread-crust morsels
        in the oil and piss street puddles,
my dream endured
        even after hollow-hearted racist cops
        beat down, put down, kick down, hurt down
        the innocent,

my dream of love endured
        in a place where the ocean surrenders
        its imagination
with open arms for the poet's lyrics,
and the flowers
        are not yours, not mine, nor property
        of the wealthy—
            but belong to everyone.

                    *   *   *

I remember at sixteen
            all that green
            floral-dressed suntanned people
            the salty humidity
                in the air
made me think L.A.
        was Eden, was where my babe and I
        would make things right,
            with Santana, Joplin and Hendrix
            kicking tunes like a dragster spinning wheels
            and drugs flowing in to heal my broken heart
            when my babe
said she didn't want me anymore
            I leaned on the piers at Santa Monica
            or hunched by the underpass warehouse
                with other splintered lives
                    picking my bloody glass memories
                        from my palms and bare feet;
my life was a bus without brakes
coming down a steep mountain road,
        hurling through the green life
        on LSD, Mexican weed, punch spiked
            with PCP,
            and all I could do was
            lean into the ocean breeze
                like a shipwrecked sail

Meeting My Love, True to My Heart and Loyal to My Soul

windily flopping and billowing
on the breezy waves,
waking up to
studio executives
jogging around heady floral-scented parks,
with the soft pat-pat of tennis balls
on tennis courts,
and beyond brown crop people
bobbing at dawn
against a blue horizon,
slaving for pennies,
absorbing the rain and wind
brown faces
emerging from orange groves,
not as troops, not as warriors,
but bridge makers,
peace menders,
friends and lovers.

Two

Lisana, your eyes, slanted up a little
with black eyeliner,
make you look like a majestic jaguar
prowling in thick jungle leaf and vine growth—
hanging out in Panhandle Park,
on a pier at Fisherman's Wharf,
in the misty dawn, staring at the indifferent sea
and gazing at Alcatraz,
feeling like a prisoner myself,
I dreamed of a woman
like you, Lisana,
with gold loop earrings, Mayan-princess face,

elegant eyebrows and brown eyes—
your power exceeds the charm necklace
made of blessed herbs and precious stones
I wore to ward off evil, made for me by a Healer Woman
in Bernalillo, and you at my side
made marked cards and crooked dice in my pocket worthless,
when you narrowed your eyes and looked into mine,
when you stroked and caressed my face
made me smile and frown,
going from kissing to arguing in minutes—
sadness in my soul when I made you look down,
holding your tears in, your lips slightly open,
your eyelashes sweeping out from your eyelids,
made me reach over and comfort you,
made me say it doesn't matter, though it was September,
you smiled and Christmas lights went on in the air,
and your smile and your white teeth
exposed an innocence in you,
like a baby jaguar gnawing at a piece of bone,
throwing your head back with your long black hair ponytailed
and it bouncing around as you laughed
sent a howl through my blood to touch and feel you,
to get nearer to you in heart and soul—
believe in me baby, believe in me baby,
people like me are as real as the holes in a fugitive's shoes
in ice-cold water
running from the dogs—
we both close our eyes,
breathing a lover's sigh and quivering a lust-thigh groan,
breathing your body scent in, the smell of tears on your cheeks—
and then your quick-flash anger, nostrils flared,
give you the appearance of a calm priestess, looking down,
older than your sweet young years.
Then, as I open my eyes, you give me that
little-girl glance, hair falling to one side, let loose from
ponytail and hanging off to one side of your face,

makes me want to tap-dance, clap my hands, baby,
to a song and tell you with trembling raging love-knotted
lonely words that I'll never break your heart.

*   *   *

Later we walk
San Francisco streets
    stopping in for coffee and cake
    taking a seat by the window.
I tell you I am from the hill country in New Mexico
    communal mailbox
    stony paths walked by grandparents and grandchildren
    for centuries
where silence pieces together the stories of lives
    like embroidered colorful squares
    into one quilt
each life overlapping and bordering the other.
    You tell me you dance, you write poetry.
    I rub my words together like a thumb against guitar strings
    my words seeking the passion and truth
    of my soul to share with you,
as lust simmers from my loins when I look into your beautiful face
the way a ruddy seaman's face on a pier simmers
    when he looks up and sees the sea storming—
like him, my heart is grub-lumber of a dying ship
    that rots in dry dock without your love.
    How small my life really is
    how little I have done
    how small my heart pounds thump/poom
                thump/poom
    thinning itself to a papery end
    of dust in the grave dogs sniff
    and leaves and grass cover, without you.

I have never known how to love.
    I have been indifferent as the cattle-car hobo

when it comes to my emotions,
my attention on grasshoppers, suns, moons,
on the deep sadness in people settled down
in suburbs
who have drawn back their lives.
That is why I love you—
you remind me of those who let go of what they treasured most
and instead teach their hands to reel in dark seasons from
        the heart
having lived it in the white fire of the wind and sail
half naked, their words ripple over
and brim the beach.

I am earth and you are water.
We have come to San Francisco to talk of love,
where houses lean
on the downside of a hill and the exterior woodwork is
steeped in another time
of crossbones and skulls.
I am a poet and the sea molts
the lost maps in the darkness of my being
that would tell you the story of my love for you,
that would tell you the story of what happened to us in
        another lifetime
when we loved each other, when we knew each other,
when we flew to the edge of the sea
                and our spirits freed themselves
                as gifts to each other.

Three

I've written poems of rain before
from the lightest turquoise-beaded spray
that even the dandelion puffs

lifted themselves to unafraid,
                    so light was it,
and of gully washers so strong
they could push a bull over, crack a tree in half, send a windmill
hurling through the air like an arrow,
                    but the rain that started yesterday afternoon
                    was one of those the soul invites
                    that comes and cleans one of sin,
                    that comes and forgives one of his wrongs—
it affected me strangely,
the rain was a purple cloth that wrapped me
in its embrace,
as if I were its lost child
                    who had suddenly met his mother on the road
                    searching for him.

Then I thought of you, Lisana,
and I lifted my face to the fine spray of rain
asking for blessings,
                    for spiritual guidance, asking the rain
                    to guide me in our relationship
                    as it guides itself down to roots
                    that need it to grow,
                    asking its guidance in my life
                    to sink itself into my bloodroot heart
                    and allow me to slake thirstily
                    and make me stay true to my heart,
          loyal to my soul,
make me blossom and allow me to rise
upward, outward, deeper
                    as our love grows
                    in all its phases of sorrow and happiness.

I hunched up in my Yankee baseball jacket,
feeling the sadness that a man feels
when over the past twenty years he's
                    disappointed his friends, wronged his heart,

spent years as a renegade rebel
reveling in the dark nights from New York to Berkeley
searching for love that would settle his stormy soul
hopelessly waiting for the dawn
when he could look out on the Hudson River
or glance over the Pacific Ocean
and feel that peace that simple truth gives one
after the illusions and feeble lies have given way.

The usual images made no sense—
the associations that rain had had for me,
metaphors of healing
and cleansing my offenses against people—no sense.

The statue saints in the cemeteries were weeping
tears of joy,
the mangy homeless dogs
howled out their gruesome, homely songs,
the fluttering of sun rays broke through the clouds,
and in this lull of light
I felt that love that comes after a war,
that peace that a soldier traveling home feels
when viewing a field filled with flowers and grass,
understanding something he cannot put into words,
something that buzzes in the heart like a bee
or hummingbird, seeking nectar
that's formed, impossibly and somehow,
from the brutal betrayals and wasted nights and days
of violence—

the rain finally came,
fluffing itself out and down like a woman
after a shower shakes her hair,
over my face, in my hands, over my body,
pausing, then reaching for me with open arms
to say in her soft way how she loves me
and how glad she is I'm finally home.

* * *

The old women from my village
would say of love that if I waited and believed, it would come
from an unlikely place and unexpected,
       Believe, they would advise, *Believe,*
         and I didn't.
With other gypsies I sat around all night
and we dreamed between outlaw rappings
of a sweet love we might one day find,
after making cold love to whores in hotels,
I'd toss and turn in the dark wondering
what was happening to me, how I never wanted to turn out this
    way,
how I'd dreamed of being honest and filled with dignity
and true to one woman,
      working out our differences and dancing in delight
      when we agreed heart-wise on things,
        and the rain finally
           glistened back to me years later
              in the dark streets
                that I'd arrived at a place
                  meeting someone
                  where it was now
                    possible.
This comes as a strange admission
to a man like myself who played the hangman's role
in life,
taking on all adversaries: I never slept,
allowed no one to enter my heart;
nor did I allow myself to even glance inside my heart
for fear of encountering the demons that haunted me
and which I'd been able to ignore and dismiss
by numbly drinking myself to a degree I could no longer
    feel anything.
It's very strange that I now open myself up
to the universe,
      to participate in the human drama

where I'll suffer and love with the rest,
where I'll wake up now with her by my side
         and feel capable of taking on any experience
         straight up with my emotions and heart and soul
         absorbing the wind, the sun, the rain,
         whirling slowly through the seasons of love with you, Lisana,
         enduring the frosty winters, the sad autumns,
         ripening richly and giving off great bounties
         of fruit and crops that I've allowed to hibernate
         which now I brim in your lap with endless harvests of
                 sincere love.

Four

I entrust my heart to you, Lisana.
Do as you wish with it. You may squeeze it
like an orange, puckering your lips,
tonguing the last sweet bitter drops
on a hot day.
You may use it like a dirt side path
to seclude yourself from the crowds
and sit on the bank staring out at the Rio Grande River,
wondering if you should give all your love to me
and become water flowing lazily downstream
to the Gulf of Mexico where you would merge
with other tributaries in their tribal gathering.

You may use it like a child uses his bicycle
on a mountain path,
bouncing off rocks and splashing through streams,
leaving it hanging on hooks in the garage
or irritable with the boring hours of summer,
purposefully freeze yourself
         and bicycle out into the December night

until your hands are frozen stiff,
your cheeks chilled hard,
but your heart is warm again.

It's stupid to offer my heart to someone
so fearlessly,
to entrust my heart to your hands,
to use it as a scarf to wipe your sweat away
when you're hiking a mountain trail,
to entrust my heart to your hands
to hold as you might your infant
and let it suckle your breast,
let it sit on your shoulder
        like a parrot
        in the black curls of your hair,
madly cawing its language of love.
Nonetheless, I leave my heart in your hands
in much the way the postman rings the doorbell
and deposits a strange package
        warning you
        if you open it, there is no turning back,
no return to sender, you must
prepare yourself
to explore the dark and bright regions
of a faraway land
carrying only your heart
as your compass,
your own heart's instinct
as your guide.
Leave behind all you've learned,
leave the house just as it was—
the bed messed up,
the pot with boiling water steaming,
the radio symphony filling the rooms,
the washed and dried clothes unfolded,
just vanish into my heart

and witness
yourself as you've dreamed it could be.

Know that my heart is a flower, the petals
of a flower dripping with rain.
I have fallen
in love only twice: both strange tides
touched me and shook my feelings
in the blue water of the lake.
My heart, a flower, tossed to the spread hands
of water.
                    Know that.

Five

Does anything matter
when we see each other
and we gather all our lonely days and nights
from the orchard's heart
like baskets of apples on a summer afternoon?
Does anything matter
when our eyes meet and we see ourselves in orchards
running under the branches,
the heavy green fragrance, the thick grass
catching at our heels,
and we remember poems by Frost
when the world seems so perfect?

Those black moons that our eyes were,
those pitchforks that our hands were,
those stalks of withering corn that our legs were,
illuminated now with dawn light
and a fine sprinkle of rain,

and we don't rush in the house for cover,
we lift our faces to the rain and stick out our tongues.

We've spent hours on the phone trying to squeeze
each other, talking of love and hopes and dreams
hoping to touch each other across the miles—
but these days not even favorite songs will do—
no amount of mind foreplay suffices to lessen our disease.
We are in love, wondering where this whirling wind of lights
spinning us will finally settle us down
and wherever that will be,
             it'll be fine with me.
             I mean, if we have no money
     no food
     no shelter
     we can start
             just by holding each other.
And this sounds strange
in a world where people marry for all the other reasons
and fall in love for even stranger reasons.
Ours is pure.
Ours is ours, is us,
is braiding you and me into one.

Six

Us in a restaurant, woman,
by the fireplace
flames are oars rowing us
as we lean over life's railing
to see the sunrise on the horizon.

The waiter brings our food
and we eat.

How young men glance at you,
their eyes pause
and breathe you in,
your arms and waist murmur like swaying flowers.
How young women brush
their hair aside to look at you,
an emerald in the swaying flames,
and the elderly recount
their youthful joys.

As we left the restaurant,
a small drizzle shook from the sky
and dazzled the silent night street.
The rain wet your lips
sloped like a rainbow
with peaceful shimmers
as your arms enclosed me and you kissed me.

We walked on and came to a night auction,
entered the house and took our seats
as a diamond ring was being passed around.
It reached us. It sparkled
in your palm, the tiny cut windows on the surface
burned brilliant flecks of light
fluttering in your eyes.

We left the auction,
preferring the infinite words
I love you and the rain.

*   *   *

I have desires to close myself up when I come so close
to you, Lisana, as though I hear your footsteps
down every corridor, doves flying outside from your passage,
and the doors of my body closing and opening
as you come closer, and along the hallway,
you understand the signs and symbols

painted on the walls, you pass each painted face of my stages,
each mean cheek and down-laden eyelid,
blood on my shirt in my warring days,
roses tumbling from my arms in love days,
you pass them to the one they tell about,
to me, who waits beyond the lit torches and cries of crowds,
who waits like fresh grass for happy feet of children,
and you scent the spring, the change of time in my words,
entering the forest my arms are
where animals talk with you,
and the sun bends to you like a servant opening its doors.

But you wonder why I'm so uncomfortable
holding hands
or why if you come up from behind me
placing your hand on my shoulder
why I get anxious—
        you wouldn't believe it, Lisana,
if I told you that with all the counselors
and therapists and do-gooders,
        millions of kids grow up never being touched
        until they're fourteen or older.
These hands were never taught by other hands to touch,
        but to deflect the blow,
        defend turf,
        flip off rich bigots,
        inflict self-destruction;
loving touch is as foreign to millions of kids
as a cold morning under warm feather blankets.

        Our hands and fingers shaped themselves,
        crooked claws for scratching concrete dust
        from cell walls to escape,
        our thumbs are bent from pushing too many
                chrome cold-water buttons in cell sinks,
        our fingers clench bars waiting for chow call
        or knot up to defend ourselves in a fight.

I once heard that a Latin American guitarist
had his fingers cut off by a dictator's militia
and still he played in a soccer field before thousands
with bleeding stubs strumming red strings
                    dripping with blood—

Imagine if you existed with half a heart,
a half-heart kid at fourteen
never having been touched in a caring manner
wondering about it as he might wonder about
                    nuclear physics,
                    wondering
about love in the same manner he wondered
how the moon held itself up so high,
                    so far away,
                    unable to touch it
                    though he wanted to with all his heart.

First time hands ever loved me,
first time I ever felt sweet sympathy for my wound,
first time I realized a hand's concerned touch
could be like a garden's flowering abundance
of loving textures, colors and aromas,
was when Sister Theo in the orphanage infirmary
placed her left hand on my thigh
and with her right dabbed iodine
with a cotton swab on my knee
scratched jumping off the monkey bars.

A massive, middle-aged Swede,
grandmotherly and vulnerable intimacy
making me feel I was her friend and we could share secrets,
dreams, her words, gestures, features cooing meekly
with care for me.

Stout, huge-armed, brawn-bodied and towering
in white nun apparel, moving thickset hips and thighs

heavily in the cramped dispensary cubby,
selecting Band-Aids and iodine from the glass medicine cabinet,
and after fixing me
and stuffing my pockets with hard candy,
    she led me out back
holding my hand, drawing me close to her
as she explained a flower's precious qualities—
her small garden
seemed physically connected to her, an extension
of her heart in her touch, scattering in me seeds of hope—
    when much later as a man
    always on a road between
        towns,
    or between relationships
    beginning or ending,
    I think of her sweet hands and what they taught me—
    my hands, like cold-weather horses,
    trudge against the harness
    breaking hard ground of words
    that now and then
    bless me with flowers in the loneliest nights.

Now, looking for words to tell you
    how I feel,
when I see you this morning, Lisana,
my heart slopes down
to its white bone-board house
where its words are small skulls
covered in hair it buries in wax
of my flesh cooled in blood.

And later that afternoon,
after you have left,
outside, leaves scribble across wind
something wild
something green
with what I wanted to say to you.

* * *

A lover must liberate his lover, free her of lies to be entirely
    honest,
a lover's heart must be a page-turner book filled with familiar
    feelings
                    of trust, dreams,
a lover's mouth must fit her mouth like two fingerprints perfectly
    matched
in a crime of obsession for each other.
                    Two lovers bring the story to life
            that resides in each other's hearts,
        and the living of those stories lifts the two lovers into
            heights where only eagles fly,
fly over different-colored skin,
            fly over different cultures,
            fly over dark and brooding days,
            fly, both of them,
                    even when she is on stage and dancing
                        she keeps him under her wings . . .
and later when she is talking to someone, she says, *Oh yes, my love
or my husband, or my sweetness,* in referring to the other half of
her heart . . .

            * * *

My loving self traced its earthquake origins.
        The earthquake threw the brown stones of my eyes
        up from dust, into the air,
        scattered my broken-backed heart of twisted rock mass
        and wove the stone into a deep solace
        of summer's unwavering gaze.
I am speaking to you about the passion that runs in my blood
        to make love with a woman
        with no bounds, inhibitions or fear—
as the inexorable colt's bounding hooves
        sprinting with the sculptor's chisel
        on barren stone, bucking and rearing
        out of passion-bleak life.

I want to sing as the million leaves
in breeze to describe my lust,
shake my slavering jowls like a stray mutt
at the water and wind and sunshine,
invent my mumbo-boogy-joogy ay-man-sighings
and romp the rules that immunize my flesh
from a woman's lust—
howl my leafed laughter and softly glide
my blue-heron heart
past the No Trespassing signs and padlocked gates
in woman's heart—
climb over the gate, cross the bridge, go down the embankment,
and following the winding path
of her breast and hips and thighs
to the path between her legs, between her soft cattails,
to her vagina—
bed shakes, earth tremors under the floorboards,
her hips shake with orgasm,
shivering trembling in our muscles,
8.0 reading, startling from her blood
thousands of snow geese
and bird-splashing landings between our thighs,
rearranging the coastlines of our bodies,
dazed, rippling new borders
where our passion passes freely to the other,
earth blowing its breath in our arms, legs, lips—
our groans,
cave talismans we shake and rattle in our throats,
expelling deep old breathing of animals,
gusting with deep organ-mouth sounds,
until we burst from the branches of our bodies,
bellying the darkness in each other,
shimmying slowly in the primal slush of our passion,
familiar to us as tulips to butterflies.

Seven

When I see you, Lisana,
snowflakes softly fall from the sky
    melting as they hit the street
    as we do
    becoming more than we are
    when our gaze falls on each other
and sitting next to me, you tremble, your loins
murmur with lust,
you break out in a sweat and tremble,
too timid to look at me, you go to the bathroom.
        Equally so,
sitting next to you,
    I feel you take me in
    like a swift traveling current
futile to fight against; I surrender
to you,
    willing to trust where you are taking me
wanting you
and not knowing where we are going.
I sense it is
a circular room with endless mirrors
each giving a distorted reflection
of us.

We walk a trail along the Rio Grande
along the bosque
we kiss and talk and sit, meditating
    on the water, Canadian geese and red-tailed hawks
    swoop and glide,

lizards skitter from brambly brush,
I love who you are,
sitting on the river's bank,
the silver twisting sheen of the river's surface
mesmerizing us
wondering what the journey holds for us,
committing our love to each other.

You are my woman
fully and completely,
even as you sit next to me,
I want to lose myself in your
brown eyes, thick black hair, legs, lips,
swirling into the silvery sheen
of water I bathe in,
in green leaves overflowing
above our heads,
be in bed with you,
indulging in your sweet loving
and deep growling teary-eyed intimacy
knotting up unraveling heart dreams.

We drive to the mountains,
you strip naked and bathe in the ice-cold creek,
and later we drive into Bernalillo and eat at the same
restaurant
where we once met,
this time the initial spark of love
is a full-blown universe of flame
we kiss in, walk in, love in,
a simmering petaled fire that spills over into all we do.

I don't want these words
to explain my love for you.
I don't want poetry to consume you,
to embark with you on an imaginary journey,

I don't want letters or kisses on paper,
    I want you in the blood and flesh.
        I don't want to think of you
        or want you
        or dream of you—I want you here
        with me,
    a man in the garden hoeing weeds, planting roses,
    raking the ground,
    wearing my sombrero—
            a rowdy bedlam of loving you
            mobs my heart
            in the garden just as a rose thorn
            sticks my thumb and it bleeds.

Eight

Lisana, in the patio,
bending in the garden,
raking and mounding dirt wells around flowers
in the sun, wearing a straw hat, halter top and shorts,
it was you who came into my life
raking hot coals of past sorrows
still embering hurts
that you cooled and doused with laughter
and your sweet touch
pruning in my soul's deepest caves
the flowers of hope that never had sunshine
but were kept alive by my own light
of faith that I would meet someone like you
one day.
It was you who stepped back and got stuck
by a cactus needle,
a single red drop of blood on the sidewalk

was a moon where my dreams reveled
in lust, wrestling with themselves
in red desires of lovemaking dreams
of you and me
from long ago,
where I swear we met once, on a stony cliff
in some forsaken and hopeless landscape,
somewhere sometime,
you and I were two birds merging into one flight,
as that day we walked in the Rio Grande brush
beneath the lofty cottonwood trees.
I thought you were so beautiful, Lisana,
as leaves whispered above us, Canadian geese
flutter-splashed in the river,
I saw us as a dreamer looking down a well,
water so pure, water so deep, at the bottom
in the sediments and grain sands
something gold shines and it's us,
dancing in the park, hugging in the streets, wherever we go,
beneath rain and under the sunshine
you are the dream I skipped to as a child playing in the dirt,
you are the dream I merrily laughed out loud at
when I was young and believed in ghosts,
you were the dream that spilled a drop of blood
on my clean white soul
one autumn day when I realized without you
my innocence was lost,
you were the dream
I told stories to in bed, I shared my soul with,
and it's the stories we become, re-creating and adding
to them as our lives develop together;
we'll lose ourselves in the stories and poems,
wondering how our lives become one,
and enter and exit one story and poem
in this mad whirling dance of love
that we've crossed from one reality into another

without boundaries or rules or laws or promises
just opening our eyes in bed
and caressing each other in bed,
kissing my cheek, me kissing your thighs,
opening you to a full-moon glow
as I devour you gently—
I lick your paws, your neck, wrestling with you
as we go into the dark sniffing
the leaves, the blood drops,
the flowers, the soil recently turned over
to ensure good solid growth.

We create our own jungle, our own rule, our own commitments,
our own world
where a drop of blood symbolizes moons, where my tears
are dew dripping and reflecting off the blood drop,
we go creating our own lives together
like the honeysuckle vines that wrap around
the volcanic rock fountain in the patio garden,
we create our love
that draws blood from your sweet flesh,
and as you wonder how we could meet, how we can love,
how we can stay together
when our cultures are so different;

you must understand that the wind whispers our names
in its stormy nights, when things call out in desperate
voices and sorrow-filled violent noises,
you must understand that just as there are seasons
to the year
we too as humans have our seasons
of drifting and settling down,
of hate and love and war and peace,
and that you and I move into the vast open space
of our lives,
creating lives together as we wish, as we work for,

as we have dreamed and told stories of and yearned about,
and did you know that in the supplest and most tender shoots of corn
the rains and snows and winds have pounded and ravaged
and hurled themselves against
and still the corn seedlings rise like courageous
rays of green light to devour the warmth
and increase their goldenness by sheer hope and deep-soul knowledge
that they must grow toward the light
and I grow toward you and you toward me,
risking being ridiculed and ostracized, risking
our hearts like trout swimming upstream
to the birthing waters, lashing like maddening waves
against the dark reef of our bones,
calling us back to our beginnings, to our original womb
where we once were one, where we once were mere specks of light
floating in the universe and by chance,
we clashed, we ignited and became spark
in the dark long journey our lives went on.

Understand, my love,
that I have seen death so many times, have been locked
up in the darkest prison cells,
that I wandered streets as a child sheltering
myself beneath cardboard boxes or wrecked junk-car trunks in alleys,
that I slept in the fields and ate leaves from elm trees,
so hungry and homeless and still I dreamed,
I kept dreaming and holding on to the deep-down dream
of one day you and me dancing beneath the stars,
in the night, holding to each other,
in bed nibbling and licking and kissing and touching and entering
every part of our bodies
in this fiery surrender called love.

Watching you out the window
scoop dirt and plant and smooth the soil,
I want to wrestle you down in the dirt,
lift your shirt and suckle your sweaty breasts and nipples,

I want to lay you flat on your stomach and mount you
and kiss your neck from behind,
run my tongue down your spine, licking the dirt-grit and sand grains
from your flesh, licking your sweat
and sucking you hard
until we emanate heat and blossoms
bursting from our mouths in orgasmic bloom
grunting and grinding and hurting with pleasure
gasping in dirt naked beneath the sun
thrashing about in the flowers
and shovels and rakes
until our lovemaking runs its current
like a soft creek bed with a trail of water
trickling somewhere in the leafy shaded area of the forest
where deer and eagles come to drink.

Ah, Lisana, you worry we are so unlike each other,
I ask you to commit yourself to me,
you worry about me being from
street-hustling corners and gangster nights,
you from horseback riding and bicycling downhill paths,
me from war zones and addictions and loose women,
you from the gentrified life
curried with schooling and reserved mannerisms,
me with outburst of gypsy songs and impromptu poems,
you with intimate whispers of loving me,
me with bear-growling lusting you,
you with your panic attacks and me with my somber moments
of sadness,
we just go, baby, we just do what we need to do,
make no promises, no commitments, reach for the other's hand
and never let go, which is good enough for us now
as we climb this incredible mountain of hope and faith
believing if we fall or slip or hurt ourselves
that the other will catch us, heal us, be there—
the two of us in this endless infinite country of things
we want to do to each other, pleasures we want to share,

dreams we want to achieve,
sadness we'll experience, sorrows
we'll endure, the two of us moving like explorers
in this incredibly beautiful wilderness
of each other's hearts,
adventurers mapping out the mysteries of each other
and along the way meeting parts of each other
we never dreamed could be so amazingly beautiful.

*   *   *

Appreciate that our lives are so brief
and that if we don't listen to the music
roaring with enchanting news of loveliness
        all around us,
if we don't calm the rage gouging gaping holes in our hearts,
if we don't take our power
        and use it to spread our arms
        and believe we can fly, believe we can love,
        believe as we did when cruising as teenagers in the park
        that love is possible,
if we don't spin in our dizzy dance
        euphorically celebrating our lives,
                our beautiful existence,
                if we don't pause on the doorstep
                each evening and look up
                at the sky
                and wonder with humble joy
                at our souls pulsing in every musical note
                of all creation that seeks to grow,
                doing our part to nourish
                        and create beauty where we can,
then we are not alive, we do not fulfill our humanness,
we do not have the right to call ourselves human.

And that's where you come in, my lovely Lisana,
woman who feeds the flames at my heels
so that at times I feel there are Eric Clapton guitars

in my veins forcing me to sometimes
stand on a moment's notice
and clap and sing and dance my happiness.
O sweetheart,
how you radiate with the morning's splendid chorus
of voices and sounds and creatures and plants
all moving toward change that makes them more
of who and what they are, toward that blown fire we call love,
which intoxicates us to abandon our worries
and anxieties and foolish whims of greed and bitterness,
stripping our skins of armor
    and filled with blind faith,
    we lunge into dark laughing
    as the rest of the living cadavers
        stare on their way to work, and banks
        and lawyers' offices,
        wondering what special spirit has possessed us,
        praying that it catches them too
        praying for a small window in their hearts to open again
        where the sun slants though
        announcing a new day,
        a dream that they too can follow
            freely, I say freely, freely . . .

Nine

This is our wedding poem, Lisana,
and I don't want to be naive about life—
Not a day passes by that I don't look up
and say a small prayer to help me get by.
Friends from 'Frisco, New York and here in Abiqui
call to share their woes and worries.
I tell them what I share with you,
how when I go running every day,

memories spark against the stones beneath my feet
and I listen to the red and yellow finches
in the brush, remembering at my grandma's porch
in Estancia how their song tunneled a ray of light in my sadness.

I see the roadrunner perched erectly on a cinder-block wall
and wish I had some bread, something to offer it
as a sign of brotherhood, but I move on,
greeting geese that float in the standing water from last night's rain.
Every raindrop that fell from the sky last night
while I slept, uncovered pebbles—opposites attract.
These pebbles and stones
make sense to me—when I work hard and wake up
to mountains of more work, I remember the raindrops
polishing the hard hot stones;
I come out and visit the stones,
their way of communal living makes room
for younger stones inching their way up from the heart of earth,
and what I want to say is that they have endured
a thousand years of struggle just to be blessed by a single raindrop,
hurling itself like a phosphorescent meteorite
splashing with such intensity against their unexpected and somber
placidness, creating delicate, mirroring lights from pebble to pebble.

And to you, Lisana, I offer these pebbles, offer you these prayers,
given to me from the stones by the arroyo where I run—
may you have the after-rain glint of joy in your laughter,
may storms give a shining wisdom that brings out the best in you,
may your love nest in the earthquake, enduring changes and
        passage of
time, and let nothing come between us
except the flower that cracks rock and makes it more
of what it was, making one stone crack into fragments
like puzzle pieces that fit the edges where your heart broke.
I offer through this poem all the blessings given to me,
from sparrows and horses and happy dogs and lizards
skittering in frantic wariness at my passing,

the prairie blossoms that have no name, the misty romantic
    drizzles
that sop my head and make me smile when I run along a river.
The hawks gliding with such effortless grace,
all of these blessings, when I was sad and confused and feeling
unloved, took me out of myself and filled me with all
they had and were, and I was just a passing stranger who went
    from sadness
to joy, from silence to dancing, from clenched fist to clapping,
from loneliness to celebrating how lovely the stones were,
how each became a step to where I was going,
how each gave me its dignity, its patience, its wisdom,
to reach this hour, this time with you, this moment of intimate
    friendship,
giving me a song from my heart to give to you
as we wed our souls.
Let us be as the stones, forever true to each other's love,
as the love we have for each other dances
like rain dances with earthquakes and the sun evaporates
the moisture from each pebble, our love will be the mist
that hangs over the canyons, slowly dissipating with the long
    day's heat,
to reveal how much more love we have for each other,
the mountain peaks go high, brothers and sisters, go high . . .
and the paths endlessly wind to illuminate our intimate journey
    together—
remember the stones, how no one oppresses another,
how there are no wars among them, how after the rain
their colors are so bright you'd think they were flowers, the hearts
of young and old lovers basking in the coolness of the dawn.

Ten

Lisana, it started with you in the garden
absorbing the warm morning sunlight
in shorts, tank top, barefoot,
      raking the moist soil
      and pulling weeds, mounding up dirt
           around the rosebushes.
      What were you thinking,
      what cool stones of thoughts washed ashore
      in your blood from loving you last night?
Those stones you circled around our rosebush
were satisfied with the deep current of our affection,
how my lips and hands and legs and arms
wash over you
      wading out into me, seeking the shallows
      where you can reach down beneath my blood
      and pick up rocks that delight you.
My blood, like any river, has gouged out pools
and cut in the banks
         remapping its journey.

None of this did I intend to say.
I want to focus on our journey together,
starting in the garden,
      starting with a seed
      in the moist soil,
      with raking the dirt smooth
      with watering the well
         with watching it from my window
           grow.

Lisana, I need to live in the country, in a cabin
where the only sounds that I hear are those of the woods and
    your voice,
my dogs groaning in their sleep—
               enough of the prattle and soap-bubble brains
that clutter my day. Friends of mine believe the world is ending,
others watch scenes on the evening news—earthquakes in Turkey,
racist assassins murdering high school kids, landslide sludge of
    drugs and booze
liquefying brains and deep-freezing souls;
    while I acknowledge this, I sweep past it like a general on
        his horse,
rearing forelegs clawing air,
    and while my heart grieves such violent madness and
        catastrophe
   what little joys I've truly cherished I hold in my palm
like a fledgling sparrow accidentally
            tumbled out of its nest—
                    into your world
brown-eyed, stout-limbed, gregarious and quiet,
a soul like a kitchen counter heaped with farmer's-market fruit
and vegetables,
    see your emotions like red and yellow peppers,
    onions of laughter that make us cry,
    beets of blood passions, carrots of quick glances,
and my soul gushes like icy river water
    over you,
        resisting nothing,
        your firm thighs and celery poise,
an abundant garden you are to me, aromatic with sage, thyme, haughty
roses lost in their beauty, keeping true their covenant
    and God's law to being themselves and praising life
    with each breath.

We don't mind getting lost on long drives
through the mountains

because we are always where we belong when we're with each other,
we don't mind the sadness that blossoms between us
because our happiness flourishes wildly around us,
entangling our feet as we lose ourselves in the mist
            of our day-by-day existence
                    holding to a dream
                    that we can be the sweet dream
                            in a world of nightmares.
I know what I'm saying.
        Having just opened the windows
        to hear the birds and inhale the dawn's spinning flash
        of light bursting,
        having separated clothes and put them in the washer,
                others in the dryer,
        letting the dogs in, romping floppy-eared gypsies,
my soul the whole while
whip-cracks with vigorous joy
        at having you in my life,
        at pointing out hills, trees, valleys,
        eating in restaurants, attending bullfights,
        turning you over and loving you hard,
        reveling in your taste, your kisses, your sweet breasts,
        all of it makes me feel like a small flower
        just surfacing from the moist dark soil
        and feeling the sun on my petals for the first time,
        makes me feel
                I don't have to own anything or make a lot of money
        just dance and sing my whole being and manhood,
        celebrating our marriage, praising your beauty,
                your gentle warrior-woman wisdom
                that seeps from your mouth and eyes and fingertips
                feeding your hummingbird-man
even as you train yourself to journey on your own road,
demanding no commitment, no plan for the future,
no predicting what or who we'll be or do tomorrow,
                the story we've unfolded is ancient,

is a myth in books young dreamers read
to find meaning in life.
I know what I'm talking about.

Eleven

Lisana, this morning celebrates our marriage
and your beauty, your eyes,
  how I saw them last night
  when running on a dirt road
  way out to be alone on winding prairie trails
to my right the descending sunlight lit the sage and grass
a dark green-gray, your eyes
  when thoughtful like two drum-skin heads
  smeared with handwork stains
  dirt-leaf stains
  hands beneath a coconut tree beating the skins
    with rhythms old as jaguars
but to my left,
running at a good pace with my blood flowing like a woman's cry
in the heat of a tribal song when she swirls in hypnotic heart daze,
to my left
your eyes again, but lime green, an airy turquoise
such a gentle, fragile, feminine lacy green,
  reminiscent of your eyes
  when they're laughing and happy,
    when you're walking at dawn among the markets
    in Mexico
  shopping for fresh fruit and a new journal,
  when you feel your heart opening
  like a nest that's always been there, and surprised,
  you find hummingbirds whirring their wings
  in your pulse.

* * *

Ah yes, this morning streams clear and cold through my blood
beckoning you
barefoot and naked to enter again and bathe
and be baptized
        but it's all so much more than this—

I peeled an orange last night after running,
sweaty, aching, my life a fiesta
        with everything I've ever done and ever experienced
flashing back to myself as a child when Grandma
hummed her tribal songs
and the earth brooded under my feet like a sleeping waterfall of stone
and dirt and trees and the wind whispered my name
and I dreamed there was someone like you out there beyond the
        mountains
out in the world somewhere
        someone who danced her pain and joy in a sacred manner,
        entering the dawn with song in her bones and muscles.

But it's all more than this.
When you lie next to me in bed,
sometimes I gaze for a long time at your hips, your legs,
your hair and eyes, your forehead and chin,
the place beneath your ears that softly runs down to your neck,
making every book and law and astute expert and scientific
        breakthrough
        meaningless,
because in moments when the sun is just coming through the
        windows,
just topping the Sandia Peaks to the east,
the only truth is you, naked, clutching the pillow to your face,
        and my small gift to you,
        as wars are declared on TV,
            interviews about AIDS and racism and starvation
            snarl on the radio,
I prepare coffee for you, toast and jelly,

unafraid of the future, even if we have no money,
no idea how to solve the problems in our relationship,
I solve it all with a cup of coffee, a piece of toast, an orange for you,
and while you eat and shower,
>I go outside to sprinkle down the garden,
>beckoning with open arms
>the coming time
>>when I can see myself again
>doing what I want
>in a city, waking up, no scripts, no book deadlines,
>reading poetry at my pleasure,
>translating poetry,
>reading your work, Lisana, shaping and structuring your poetry,
preparing your poetry manuscript
>like this garden,
>letting the lilac and sage and roses
>>whirl on the air
>as if they were you on that wooden floor in that building
>>in New York
>>>ecstatically with lifted arms and crouched pelvis and
>>>>bent legs
>>>doing what your heart wildly dreams of doing.

But now I run the winding roads
where I haven't been before, alone, my heart beating hard,
my legs lifting me up the hills,
my breath heaving even and with the effort of a man always
pushing himself harder,
>knowing there have been easier ways to do things
>but I never took them—
I was once a butler, an actor,
an elephant trainer in a parade in an Iowa town,
a flamenco dancer, a bartender in the mountains of Spain,
>but my vocation now is your lover man,
>a linguistic archaeologist rooting out hidden words to
>>convey my love
>to you, my hate my sorrow my joy of the journey

that has me starting out early in the mist, the dark,
in the cool dawn,
feeling God in the ditch bank and alfalfa fields and corrals and horses
reminding me of those
      early dark treks as a child alone on the streets
      when home was where I sat anywhere anytime,
      but now, the flamenco dancer dances again in me,
      the singer sings again,
      my hands clap with each pulse,
      and I smile as the sun rises over the Sandia Peaks,
my words honed and carved and whittled to praise a woman like
      you
with as much fervor and compassion
as a monk praying at dawn before Christ on the cross,
with as much attention to detail
as the artist who paints the folds in the cloak of *La Virgen de Guadalupe,*
with as much humility as the common pebble,
and all the stars flicker
      in the night sky
      reflecting only a corner of the light I offer you
radiant with flashing sunlight
      dizzying and subdued as love's turns tend to be,
smoky emotions that you inhale between us,
      I lick your saliva in a kiss,
      I nibble your nipples,
      I kiss your thighs
as if composing a poem to you,
      how beautiful and lovely a woman you are.

      This morning I awake and gaze out the window
and know with a great heft of emotion in my heart that what we do
is real,
      how I know looking out at the mountains and treetops
      what we share
      is real,
      is love, is us, is you and me in our dance
      ordained by the angels and all small creatures of life

and how I want to weep thinking of you, weep because my life
    with you
is a testimony to my happiness
living with you is
my heaven, my reward for having suffered and worked and
    dreamed
you are what God has brought to me
    and my voice low and rough and gruff speaks aloud
your name
    the way a man who is prisoner in a war camp
    utters the word of his hometown,
    his wife, his guitar and music he loves,
so I stand, turn the music on, clap my hands and dance,
dance the way a pig adjusts his weight to sink deeper in mud,
I growl and bark as I turn on the shower,
I grunge down,
    fattening myself on the sweetness of our love,
    on your beauty, inward and outward,
then step into the shower, ahhh
cooling the fever of seeing you a sweet prairie dove,
    in every flower and dirt grain
        I hear the universe call my name
        and I answer it with words, I love you.

✳　✳　✳

Running late afternoon,
far out to the southwest, storm clouds
gather darkly on the horizon
and a voice in me warns
turn back,
    but I keep running
as wind blows brooding clouds over me,
thunder crackles,
and just as I top the last hill,
    sprinkles spatter the earth.
    I pause, look around, wonder if I should go back,
    but

invigorated by blustery gust, then the hushed pall,
everything shades,
the ground, normally parched dust
and black volcanic gravel
        from the dormant volcanoes
        to the west nearby,
freckles wet with raindrops,
        and my soul stands alone in the wind, rain and storm clouds
        a lighthouse in the dark,
when all of a sudden
        clouds break in an angry thunderclap,
        wind blows rain, big teardrops sting my skin,
        make me turn and sprint down the long hill as fast as I can,
inhaling sage smell, hot ground moistened
like wet jeans on an ironing board the iron
steams off;
        the smell of drought
        was the smell of my grandpa's skin,
        the smell of rain
        was the smell of my grandma's pinto beans
                in the pressure cooker in the kitchen,
        the smell of sage and hot stones cooling
        was the smell of
        a five-year-old snot-nosed boy on the prairie
an innocent time before I knew cities existed,
when I believed angels
were hawks, horses and goats,
content to wake and play in weedy fields,
antagonize red and black ants
        and step on anthills,
        escape from bumblebees in cactus blossoms—
        I inhale hard, sneakers crushing volcano dust
I dash down from the angered rain,
        inhaling/exhaling,
the silvery downpour
shakes memories in me like salmon starting to bite,
whiplashing over the water as I reel them in,

but they escape from my cracked leather doctor's-
    bag heart
    I carry day to day, town to town and door to door,
    healing the ailing in me.
Rain hurts my skin,
    my shorts and T-shirt are soaking wet,
    my blue YMCA sweat-stained cap sopped.
I lean my head from the white hail,
my memories tremble flaring aflame,
        flickering in the very cold rain,
playfully I leap to miss the drops
as I race windblown tumbleweeds
skipping beside me and outrunning me easily,
    and I proclaim the rain the winner,
        the tumbleweeds second,
    and me third, raise my arms to the sky
    as if I'd won, because I'm still a boy on dusty roads,
    running in the rain.

Later this same night
after reading poems to a group of high school kids
at an alternative school,
    I tell this nosy guy that my life as a poet
    is simply patching up the boat
    that Homer and Mayan and Aztec poets made
and set out to sea, and after decades in the storm,
discovering new lands,
the next poet steps to work on poetry and patches it up,
varnishes the boards,
mends the sails,
    sets it out to sail again,
    then the next poet steps up to work on poetry and fix
        the rudders,
    oil the motors,
    patch the dream ship,
to make it seaworthy again into people's hearts—
    I come after Neruda,

when the ship got caught in the reefs and beached,
I stay out twelve hours a day
fixing, patching the dream ship, working on a metaphor,
    arranging words,
so the poem sails safely through rough seas.

This poem is intended to be a love poem to you, Lisana—
remembering when we climbed the mountains at Canones,
when my hand grabbed a cactus
    and you pulled out the needles,
    when you taught me how to walk the sandy mountains'
        sides,
    when I learned your love for solitude
    and country air
and unbroken views of land that extended forever,
telling about times you were working at Boy Scout camps
where you had your first beer, your first boyfriend,
your first lay,
    and in this love poem, I offer you dirt roads
    to run on and get caught in the rain,
    and time to mend the dream ship.

Twelve

We have a family. No walls to keep out the stars. No rooms to
    belittle each other, shrink our
lives in dough balls suspended on hooks of jobs and lifestyles.
    We have a family.
I kiss my daughters and embrace them, share my feelings on earth
    with them,
tell them how trees talk, how plants hurt, how the sky is charged
    with gods.
I tell them the sun is a symbol of power, how if one is quiet and
    observant,

one can learn to read the stars, know the meaning of light
     radiating from the sun.
How the moon tells secrets about the bear and elk. And I need
     no medicine cards
except my own heart to tell what I know, keep what I can for my
     own spirit.
          I have a family now. The children have cast their image on
               my tongue,
and I learn daily, tell the truth, as it is. Lisana has taught me that
women are special, their bodies are like natural spring waters.
When I go walking now and see a rugged field, black birds
     swoon in,
fold and unfold on the air in airy lakes of black, I think of
     woman's lust.
I taste the dust of the day on my lips and think how I am no
     longer
the vociferous warrior, the one who howled challenge to authority.
I am learning gentleness, learning to listen to the heart more,
a tree owl listening to the darkness, plucking a noise from the
     wild grass.
          I see my own death in the blushing cheeks of my daughters,
               and utter
endless spasm of unflexing silliness of being I will float in
     someday,
the immense and deep warmth of sleep that falls over a country
     porch
on a summer afternoon is my own being. I shed the house of this
     body
I have bruised, pit against opponents, loved furiously with. And I
     hope,
equally, to use my voice and mind to support life on earth, for
     myself,
for my children.
          With you, Lisana, here in this house, as my two babes sleep
               in their room
and you sit at the table with your friend reading tarot cards,
watching you, I promise, I will live as a good man you can trust.

I cook breakfast for my friends—eggs, chili, potatoes,
buttered toast. Nothing fancy or exotic. And then tea.
A late breakfast—about eleven A.M. Everyone gets up
with dreams in their faces, the brown leaf of a tree
rooted in a star still clinging to their cheeks. A bird
on my daughter's shoulder, its wings reddening as she
speaks, and its white feathers drifting off from her lips.

I remember my dream and slowly return,
through the stone hallways of an ancient
pyramid. My face is a smoldering torch extinguished by
a blue-sky cap. A tent is set up on a sandy hill, and all
around me those Jewish priests in long black robes are carrying
rifles. War. Currents of smoke drift randomly from artillery.
I walk over the cold kitchen linoleum, hard as the blue metal
of empty shells. And then I kiss my daughters, and truly love them
another instant in my life.

Frost on all the windows turns my house into a canyon in Cochiti.
The spoon I stir my coffee with is the hardened
artery of mountain blood. I smell flint on my hand.

Lisana is a dream within a dream a thousand years from now. In
        her brown sweater,
blue corduroy pants, black boots. A refreshing break in the forest,
her body a waterfall covering me with kisses. And then my
        neighbor's rooster crows,
its song a handful of spears thrown across the field. I am very
        happy to be alive.

＊　＊　＊

This morning the rooster crowed by my window. I thought of
        the biblical
story of Christ . . . the betrayal, when the cock crowed three
        times. My eyes

adjusted to the dawn darkness of the room. The white walls were
    blue. My
pants and shirt rumpled on the floor were dark shadows.

When I took the trash out to the barrels this morning, geese flew
    in the
blue sky. The wet-rained earth exhilarated me. Puddles. By the
    leaning
rusty fence, strutting in the gray weeds, a golden hen led her
    plump blond
chicks into the year-old manure heap. Somewhere in the
    cottonwood tree,
a woodpecker played his drumstick beak against the bark skin.

The day belongs to feather beings. I sense a celebration among
    them,
each according to their custom. There is music, food, dancing,
    flying,
old acquaintances renewed. A few days earlier, when the mean
    rainstorm
had passed through here, I found soggy nests in the backyard
    grass. A batch
of weed, twigs, feathers, lint, mud, grass clippings, weed fuzz and
    chips of bark.

All the trees have fallen into a mad trance. Colors burn to
    extreme yellows,
blues, grays. Across the fields, shadows section off and catch my
horse, half in bay, auburn, and half in dark brown. Sunlight and
    shadow
halve his body. My house is a nest today as we burrow in this
    adobe home,
like earth animals, trailing in mud, calling for food, nuzzling each
    other;
the baby giggles, Lisana rocks the baby in her arms while I sit here,
recording the miracles on this November dusk.

Thirteen

A hundred yards beyond my house
the Rio Grande's cottonwoods
burst with gold. Leaves fly through the air—

> dusty air, as if the winds were trail busters,
> old exhausted cowboys
> driving invisible herds of dead buffaloes
> stampeding treetops.

Leaves
explode in the air and swirl down
like golden raindrops
flooding dirt streets,
puddling in doorways and collecting in roof wedges.

> When asked
> > *Where do you come from?*

I want to say I was born
from a leaf in the bosque.
On a November afternoon like today
my soul was formed in the mad swirlings of dying leaves
shattering against a rickety post fence,
dispersing over the barrio
to crumble and rot in the earth.

> But I am locked in by my flesh—
> by the walls and doors
> of my house. Here I cling

to my family, to this house,
to the fence they know
and words they know are mine, I cling
fighting off the autumn winds and cold—

O, but just to let go,
to let a roaring dawn take me
and fling me over the river, blow me back
and find myself floating on the brown water
toward nowhere—
        to die, to renew myself
        in black bog—
uncurl my eyes again like two buds
to light again!
Green tongue veined with maps
insects eat through, spiders web, caterpillars chew—
until one day I awake a butterfly
letting my daughter chase me
through an alfalfa field as she does now.

*   *   *

        My oldest daughter is good at getting up early
by herself,
high school friends, basketball,
            she strides out an affectionate warrior
            into a pine forest of youthful dreams bending under
                branches
                laden
                with eagle nests.
After I've showered and prayed,
I wrestle my youngest awake, and slower
            than seedlings rise through moist soil,
            she stretches, yawns, hates school,
                hates studying, brilliant
                and way ahead of kids her age,
                sees school as wasting valuable time
                when she could be playing Nintendo,

Rollerblading,
                playing basketball,
                        watching TV,
she could easily be a physician or scientist,
but I warn her not to chase money—
                chase a dream, like underwater photography
                or hiking,
                build your own boat and sail around the world,
                serve and protect the earth,
                        that's the kind of stuff brilliant
                        minds pursue,
                                not moneyed soul-shrinking
                                        status shit—
                                integrate your heart and soul
                                into your walk, talk, hands and
                                        thrust
                                        your voice
                                        up to the sky
                        as you sing your life out
                        pure, free, hard and strong
                        against any wind.
But I say none of this
as I pull her from bed,
hoping I can get her to school on time—
                a grand achievement all its own
                and equal to walking on Mars.

Fourteen

I've done some gardening most of my life. Just last week I was at
        the mall
collecting sage, and the security patrol pulled up behind me.
He asked what I was doing and I told him. I clutched a swatch of
        sage and

approached him, offering it up to his nose to smell. He drew
     back, complaining,
I know what it smells like— and I guess it was okay that we were
     stealing sage
from mall property, because he drove off shaking his head.
          Joe was with me. He makes prayer sticks, one prayer stick
               every day until he's made one
for every day in the year. It's centering work to enter into the
     light that unwhirls from his
fingertips at some point in the Dance.
          So poetry is for me.
          I know sometimes it's distasteful and harsh, the kind of
               poetry that can
never sit in a classroom chair and listen to the teacher—it's on
     the table,
under the chair, dancing on the seat. But cageiness it doesn't lack,
     enthusiasm
for the world brims over its hands and mouth and legs.
          This last weekend I took my two daughters and two friends
               up to Creede,
Colorado. We four-by'd up an impassable switchback deep-cut
     gully-rocked elk
trail strewn with fallen tree trunks strong storm winds had
     knocked over.
Finally at the base of the peak, after passing two rushing streams
     where we
thought the Jeep would flip over, fishtailing through a mud field,
     inching
along steep downgrades, sharply up ascents that had the nose of
     the Jeep pointing
at the clouds, we found ourselves at the base of the peak, amazed
     like five lost
wanderers, staring openmouthed at the waterfall coming out of
     the side of the
mountains; elk droppings, beaver houses, bear prints, a quietness
that reminded me of a womb, or the moment when a child first
     sounds words—

I knew then I came from fish, originated from trout, that I'd been
        born from
that waterfall, pouring out gushing its jaguar tongue as if all in
        nature were
its cub, even me
        and I gasped inside my heart
while my kids scrunched through soft waist-high grass—
I looked at them in the distance tramping down to the streams,
I looked at the mountain
at the meadow
        and felt a huge urge to weep in that instant,
        to find myself in this cold hour
                surrounded with so much beauty.
That's why I guess I'm partly angered at myself
        for sweeping life away from me
        the way a drunk hurls everything off the table
                with his forearm
        that's why I respect these quiet friends of mine who spend time
whittling and wrapping threads
                around prayer sticks
that's why I go to continuing ed to workshop with welfare
        adults,
to see that waterfall pour from their mouths,
to witness the bear appear at the mouth of the red caves of their
        hearts,
to see words leap like trout from their hands and eyes
        that we cut and gut
                and fry because we're hungry,
                        we want to eat the words,
                        the bones and all,
                                spitting out the spines
                                that cats can carry off and meow Gregorian
                                chants on rickety picket fences
                                like choirs of homeless children
                                licking their paws
                                        as they pad into the world

                              made of dark alleys
                              and fish spines.
It's a good feeling when I'm washing clothes
to turn the pockets out
and see how they've filled with pine needles
dirt, leaves, sticks and pebbles
              that somehow my daughters
              out in the world collected.
It's a good feeling to cook up tamales
steaming hot, watch my girls
       scarf them down, leaving the brown corn-leaf wrappers
on the table,
         standing in the kitchen I realize after they've gone
         how I give them stories,
              how cooking tamales for them
              is a story they'll carry as a legacy
                     to define their father.
Going back to me standing at the serene pool
in the mountains,
         at a place where white-rush headwaters calmed
         my blood blending into watercress
                              algae
                                   smooth river stone
                                   elk hoofprints
         snapping back my pole to hook brookie after brookie
         wriggling, flailing, fighting to the last,
                              I knew what it felt like
                              getting hooked
                                   like that—
inside the poem,
my flesh pine bark,
              orange pectoral, pelvic and anal fins
              rise on my skin,
                     like the sound of a flute
                     coming from a treetop somewhere
                     with such nostalgic notes

Meeting My Love, True to My Heart and Loyal to My Soul   115

that my heart thinks of its loved ones
             and drops its sword and shield
and returns home
leaving the war grounds empty.
Inside the poem,
I return to a time where
I am a wisp of water grass wavering to the current
of blue summer days going downstream,
        fading as violin strings weep happiness
        I am in the poem of this meadow
meandering my way over the rocks and turns of life.

Fifteen

Lisana, you say you need time alone,
and so I pour
a glass of wine for us,
emptying what was left in the bottle.
In the cabin, you on the sofa,
I in the chair,
we gaze out the large cathedral windows
facing the full moon on the mesa,
holding hands in silence,
wondering about our future,
                        fighting against admitting
                        we are drifting apart.
It's November, a time of departures,
when cottonwood leaves sign *adios*
to the kind season,
each golden leaf a letter of regret and love
floating in the black glistening canyon creek
whirling with
the pain of our leaving and how
hard I'm going to miss you.

Our love leans and tugs,
spins, marches, sways and kicks high,
submits, controls, lifts, and finally
never created what it promised to
and what we dream it should have been.

I'm supposed to say I know it's better this way,
but I won't—
I'm the type of man
who refuses to surrender to what people expect.
I sift dust in the ruins of the deserted village
on top of the mesa,
discovering fragments of pottery shards
I bring back to the cabin
and imagine the pieces back together.

I watch crows fly across fields at dawn,
thinking of us holding hands
by moonlight,
and know that as crows serenade the chill breeze
that climbs loose rock and sandy shale sides of the mountain
to converse with ancient spirits,
the fire's flames in the Kiva dance shadows around us,
conversing with my heart
that being with you is what awakens me
to the task of true loving.

You hesitate to believe in miracles,
yet I know as I fix the fence post,
my hands clutch the shovel roughly
and as I work, there are other hands in me
filled with exuberance for life
and they push out in all directions
like roots that break bowls at the base.

✳ ✳ ✳

I don't belong to those artsy patrons in Santa Fe,
buying off poets with their money,
adult children still nursing
on baby-formula trust funds
silencing and taming the rebellious poet
into tourist-store plants decorating
quaint cafés on the plaza.

My attention instead belongs
to those garbagemen who pick up curbside trash cans
and I note how strong their hands are,
sentimental about baby strollers and black-and-white TVs
they keep to take home,
discarded by suburban wives with fingers knotted joints
harboring discontent.
        Nuns stride to mass, and their hands
        have a nostalgic sadness to them,
long lifelines, a sweet arthritic longevity
that once melodically wiped my mouth of jelly,
slapped me when I picked my nose,
pulled my ears, made me zip up my fly,
stopped me from sucking my fingers,
caught me wrapping my fist with boxer's tape,
made me wash off inked initials on my hands
copied from Cagney movies,
smacked my hands with a ruler when I threw fingers
at the liver-spotted Irish priest,
his hands raising the chalice of wine
trembling to his wrinkled lips,
he sipped the blood of Christ mumbling Latin blessings
behind the jewel-studded chalice,
placing the host on my tongue at the communion railing,
when even then I refused to let my boy-song betray
                                        my heart,
and now decline to let my poem slither on its belly
when it's so robust and loves life so much—
        my poems thrive on appreciating

the waitress serving food all day
to save enough money to buy her son
his first new baseball glove for Christmas.

Or watching the South Valley farmer's market
rickety beat-up trucks line up
stacked with local growers' fruits and vegetables,
and seeing shawled Chicanas
lean over tailgates pressing
late-autumn fruits
as if they were scoring tentative notes
        on piano keys
        of music I clearly hear,

so too my love for you
       now in the dark, illuminated by moonlight,
       as you unfold your fingers from mine,
       holding your palms up
       like moons in the dark,
       descending behind the rim of my heart
          as I ride away.

Sixteen

Lisana, this morning you walk to school
in the fruit-fragrant morning, the misty
humid air,
the forest's luxurious leafage,
the sparkling dew on stones and steel
    encircle you
    as if you were a dark emerald on a ring.
There are ghosts that reside
in the eyes of dogs,
and each leaf is a tongue chattering with wind

about whose wife is loving another woman's husband,
here at one in the afternoon it pours
love songs to you from me,
>I touch you
>I see you
>I kiss and hold and hear your sweet voice
>I pray for rain each day at one
>>to convey my passion to you
>>to douse you in my passion
>>to sop you in my joy of having you
and with the millions of eyes of rain
I see you through the open-air windows sitting in a classroom
watching me, thinking of me,
>the far undulating fields bloom
>blossoms of white fog
>and your mind and heart lose themselves
>in the constant humming of rain and mist and fog,
>walking with me, seeing my face, kissing my lips,
>my land, my love, is creating in you
>our story, our life together,
>the rain is telling you
>>the folklore of our journey together,
>>the roof dripping rain whispers
>>how we walk streets in New York,
>>the dripping from leaves
>converses with you in hushed intimacy
>how we sit before a fire in a cabin
>here in my land of *Nuevo Mejico*
>>and how we laugh, cry, quarrel,
>>>but always love,
>>>because
>people here believe in folklore,
>believe in myth,
>believe that dreams are the language of our ancestors
speaking to us, sometimes warning us,
other times celebrating a child's birth,
and when you hear thunder and lightning

in the distant sky, it is
just an afterthought of mine, my love,
something I forgot to tell you,
that I love you, it thunders that I love you
                                in lightning flashes.

Seventeen

Benito took you to the train station yesterday
at four-thirty.
I felt clear, cool, cold tears
weigh me down
the way a prisoner feels when his wife leaves
after a visit,
        a familiar feeling of water grooving
        a stone it's dripped on for ages.
This poem is about perfect mornings—
how we made love
with sunlight spreading over us
from the open window to the east,
how the old radio with the CD player
I'd bought years ago
            hummed out burning love songs—
we were like
            the notes
                    swirling up into air
                    caught
in light rays
shattered with effusions
of light
like
luminescent
rainstorms
over our naked flesh

glistening with sweat.
So much happened while you were here
making time a quartz
burn-glowing our love into a rainbow around us.

You returned, loaded down with red backpacks,
            looking weary being a month away,
features drawn tight against facial bones
                        with worry
doubting our love, having tasted men's mouths
and lips and tongues
stinging with lust and tequila
                        and I wondered
if you'd been true.
        But it didn't matter in the end,
the night of your arrival
        we quarreled
wept, accused, forgave,
                    numb from hurting love,
                    unable to relax,
threatening to leave,
sleep in another room, even going as far
as getting up
and printing out work on the computer.

        Love makes so little sense
        gives us a dog's mind and cat's heart
reduces our lives to wrecked cars
rusting in fields of yellow flowers.

It became a perfect morning when we woke up
apologizing, making lust-grunting love,
        the music on the battered jam-box
        soothing out melodies that make us grind
rhythmically
harder

wet sheets
       your face sensuously aglow
       with unfurled pleasures
        almost
            I wanted to say
            like orange trees at sunrise
            in Fort Lauderdale, Florida,
but more like the Daytona 500,
with all them cars roaring at the starting line
and nothing but black tarmac and open road.
       You kept
       wishing you could record our conversations,
       our words blushed with rainbow hues
       shimmered in the air a moment
           and faded into endless blue horizons
           of the heart.
Too bad I had work to do,
wishing it could have been another time
when Ralph flew in from Simi Valley,
       Greg from Dallas,
       Benny from San Jose,
all of us pounding out the outline for a script daily
tense, frustrated, methodically like an army
           taking a hill under great loss,
           we emerged one by one after each day
           sullen, exhausted,
             carrying another man up that hill.
You mulled on the bed, reading Neruda, Hemingway,
    on your stomach, legs crooked, heels swinging
behind you, swaying;
    later you exercised,
walked in the Rio Grande bosque
           beneath cottonwoods
gypsy dancers
           frozen in time,
           caught by the river spirit's green eyelids
           lisping, then seething its

immortal wind song.
I do not make up our love—
     I don't make up stories about it—
     what I say is true—
               this really happened—
three nights ago
we drove to my village, visited
     the shack I grew up in,
     no larger than an ordinary bedroom,
     now forty years later smothered in green leaves and trees.
I was going to go in my grandma's house;
her sixty-five-year-old son,
the town wino, my uncle still living there
     had his bicycle and weed cutter
     in the yard by the door,
        but I couldn't bring myself to go in—
        he would have cried
            and cried to see me,
               thinking, as he did,
               that I was dead.
We went over to the pond
and I sat on the picnic bench
remembering when I came here as a child
with my grandpa.
A spout of water
        curlicued up
                  from the natural springs
                  filling the pond slowly.
Under a red full harvest moon,
I recalled my childhood
when I heard a voice—
        it came from the air behind me—
        Drink the water.
        Go drink the water.
After I had,
     mystified by the voice,

it came again,
   No, no, baptize yourself
   with the water,
   for you have endured the journey,
   you are almost at its end,
     the circle is closing.
I went up to the water,
daubed a cross with handfuls
of the sweet water,
and as I sat down,
   a white shroud appeared at my right,
   a white blur in the dark,
then immediately
I saw it was
an owl
its underwing all white
not a whispered wing beat
or flutter flap
perfect silence
it appeared
its wing almost touching me
its sharp beaked head turned
toward me
and then the voice from its eyes,
   Your journey is almost over,
   you're closing the circle,
   you've survived it . . .
and it glided up to a tree branch
as I stared after it,
thinking how my grandmother had said
she would stay with her son until he died,
remain his soul companion,
   in the spirit form
   of an owl.
I drove back and we made love
in the Shafer Hotel in Mountainaire.

Serious love—
    blood pulse-b.b.,
            binging
            against my tin-roof heart
            and afterward,
when I woke up
at dawn,
        I felt it was another perfect morning—
pulling out from the parking lot,
in the barbershop
the barber was cutting another man's hair
and Lisana, you commented on how men are intimate with one
        another
when getting their hair cut,
        how true, I thought, and it felt special
        just to be alive, riding through the mountains
        toward home, as a man, a poet
                who hadn't had a job in twenty years,
                somehow I'd made it through the hard times,
                having had the experience with my grandma
                at the pond made it all worth it;
                having a beautiful woman at my side
                who, while I drove the open prairie road,
                        went down on me,
                                and I erupted as I came
                                into thundering laughter,
                                        laughing so hard
                                        with such soul-cleaning
                                                clear-sighted love of life
                                                sensations so roller-coaster
                                                        thrilling
I laughed, laughed, laughed, laughed
holding the wheel,
                my head tossed back,
                feeling so good with so much love and life
                and things going good for me

                for miles I laughed
                    and laughed
made it all worth it
so good to find myself a poet
on this perfect morning.

 Afterward, we packed a picnic sack
with fruit and sandwiches and a bottle of wine
and went to the park.
There is so much we don't know about ourselves.
But we learn.
        A man at the park,
        in T-shirt, jeans, pudgy, middle-aged,
        set gallon plastic bottles of bleach and milk
        a mustard one
                    with a squirt nozzle,
                    a brush and rag
                        on the table.
        His small, shaggy white dog
                    on the table
                    surveyed the park.
I thought they were going to picnic together—
        instead, he shampooed, soaked and scrubbed his dog on the
            bench—
munching my sandwich, sipping wine
                    with you, my beautiful girl,
                    the sight looked lovely
                    under the trees
                    on a Sunday evening,
the man bathing and toweling his dog
was a fine thing to do.
When I asked you, Lisana, if you'd date such a man,
They hurt too easy, you said.
        And I could understand how they could, these men
        who love their dogs and take them out on Sundays
        for a bath at the park.

                        *   *   *

A gust shook the elm trees
as if reading omens in the green leaves,
and I thought how
the break in the branch
carries the story of storms.

We don't stay home alone
or spend our weekends washing our dogs.
We go out, get drunk, we fight, lie, fuck
                    and betray ourselves.
We become worldly, and we brush off the betrayals
from friends, keep at bay
any intimacy, always plan for escape,
                    lying to ourselves
                    that it's the life we wanted.
No commitments,
no connections,
no convictions,
no empathy,
no trust,
no vision—
            we keep hoping for something better
            to turn the corner on an ordinary day
            we keep thinking that what we have
            is not good enough,
            that hurt is to be buried, never talked about,
            that we must indulge in pleasure
            even if our heart is not into it,
            forbidding anyone inside our intimate secrets,
            pursuing our illusions
                    avoiding the simmering, volcanic flowing
                    of our hurtful memories.
We prefer denial, teasing of artificial
love, samplings of lusty nights,
        but to seriously stand the line
        seems beyond us.

I told you, Lisana, that
in our wounds our powers
                              reside,
               when you dance, remember
               when you were with your horses,
               remember the nights when you were the only one
               in the world giving your life
               to becoming one with your horse,
how you sat in the stall, leaned against the wall
and watched your horse eat grain and alfalfa,
the size of your loneliness
seemed larger than the world,
               but your dream to be the best
               compelled you
                              through loneliness,
                              and the woman you are
               carries in her the horse's waking gallop,
               the horse's robust vigor at dawn,
               the horse's truth and loyalty,
               even shedding blood, scarred,
                              you remain so much more beautiful
                              for doing what you did
               because you believed in it.
               I told you when you dance,
when you move across the stage,
when you want to express yourself truthfully
and connect to the universe,
               think of the horse and yourself,
think of those nights all alone
               while the world beyond you
               seemed to be enjoying itself
               and you seemed to be losing some essential joy
               to life,
               but it wasn't so, my love,
               it wasn't so—
                              the sun and moon burned bright
                              in your relationship with the horse,

Meeting My Love, True to My Heart and Loyal to My Soul

squirreling around those barrels,
the arena became your universe,
and beauty sprouted in every tight-hoofed stop
        and head-rearing halting,
beauty rampaged through your woman heart,
beauty spewed forth in the dust clouds,
in the immeasurable ecstasy of you and the horse
        becoming one
on those glorious nights all alone in the arena.
You were riding God,
    you were a goddess,
    and no one understood it but you and the horse,
    no one knew the reins were winds,
    the muscles in your thighs were stormy hurricanes,
    the jolting takeoffs, the turns, the cutbacks,
    were all some marvelous ballet dance
            connected to earthquakes
            and fertile lowlands
            where crops grow the best,
no one knew
    that your loneliness poured out
    when you brushed down your horse, when you unsaddled it,
    you were unburdening yourself
        of your own despair and doubt,
    and riding that horse
    you had a place to stand in the world,
    a place to speak from,
    a place to root in and grow from,
            the horse was God's womb,
            the manure heaps were God's womb,
            and you were in the fiery sublime light of creation
    and feeding more fuel
    to light the world with your heart's love
        and your commitment
                and conviction.
So when you whirl and turn and stretch, remember
        do it with the nights and days

of you on your horse in mind,
racing like lightning
    shuddering the air
    your heart beating
          love-life
          love-life
          love-life!

Eighteen

How a wife packs a lunch of favorite foods
for a husband leaving to serve military duty
for his country in a war,
    take this poem with you
    to remember me.
Read it around the campfire after trekking ten miles
with a sixty-pound backpack,
    hold this poem in your hands, sweet woman,
    let it kiss your sore ankles,
    let it caress your calves,
    let it befriend your heart like an unbloomed rose
    cultivated in my heart and uprooted
        to find nourishment
        and bloom in your gaze and touch.
Compare me to the stones,
the heat, the endless bleak miles,
those things that induce pain, yearning for other things,
yearning for other places,
    I offer you through this poem
    no water or rest or comfort,
just a kind of truth as the boulder that is loyal
to the desert landscape,
this is one poem-stone loyal to the landscape
of your heart, in its alternating blistered-hot days

and flesh-trembling cold nights,
        this poem-stone
        has been here for a long time.
I tell you, take this with you, use it
to spark against flint to start fire
then carry that fire into the darkness you encounter,
hold this poem in your hand and get a feel for the lay
of my heartland,
sense in it the thousands of years I have loved you,
how I have waited in this place,
        acclimated to thirst,
        to loneliness,
        accompanied by moon, sun, stars, wind and silence.

Then throw it away,
let the dusty wind cover it up again,
        and someday the unsuspecting hiker's boot
            will uncover it,
            appreciate it,
            and she will value its color, its form, its hardness,
            its truth,
            and she will put it in her mouth and suck it
                and it will quench her thirst.

Book III

La Guerra

One

I'm restless,
listening to piano recitals
accompanied by flutes,
     but they still don't distract my thoughts
     from you—
               indeed they are with you away
               on the beach with your strong legs,
               your life-loving laughter—
it is so dry here
that even the lizards scrap over dew drops,
have that mean pirate's glare to their parched eyes,
     but still I love the arid heat,
     the prairie that hasn't had rain in months,
     has me looking out my window at the volcanic rock mesas
               thinking that while you're inundated with rain
               I'm praying for even a light spray.
This thirst connects us,
what I lack and what you have too much of
               brings us together,
               opposite landscapes
                    we live in, collide in us
                    both sizzling yearning for wet love in you
                    and cracked-clay yearning
                         that rises in me
                         like dirt clouds, the breeze sweeps up in
                              cones
                         from farmers' fields,
               blowing the dirt in clouds miles away
               where water brings it down to earth again
               and quenches it, seeds it, nurtures it.

But perhaps this is good, I mean our distance from each other,
for it teaches us to wait for what is good,
wait for who we care about,
wait for the one love that is special,
            and maybe this waiting is the incubation period
            that the seeds of love we've planted in our hearts
            need to really grow strong.
I don't know if that's true,
but I do know, being the gardener that I am,
            if I were to dig up the green chile seeds
            I planted yesterday to see if they've opened,
            I'd destroy any chance of their growing—
                  and I guess, in this raging
                  fuck-as-you-will age,
                        a chance at genuine love
                        is what I'm all about.

                  *   *   *

This morning I went out
to water the garden,
      stripped rose petals
      and stuffed them in an envelope to send you,
yellow, red, pink, light blue, white—
spiritual bruises
one absorbs loving
strangers we met in bars
and went to bed with
      and in the middle of the night
      while they are still sleeping
      we covertly leave
      a part of our innocence behind like cigarette-ash burns
in the sheets.

As the years pass,
ex-lovers hold a strange place in our mind—
we believed our lover could fulfill
our yearnings,

blush the dying light of each day
with the rose's fragrance—
I don't want to sound
feebly romantic
but what I say I believe in my heart, that is,
what these petals do is
absorb the light from our loves
    in their leaves,
      yellow for happiness we had
      when we walked down a dirt path under trees,
      red is fury for the burning of our dreams
how against our better selves,
    we couldn't stop
    each morning taking a handful of a dream
        like sage and burning it,
          the blue-gray soul smoke
          veiling the blue sky
            with our loss.
But no, I'm not saying what I want—
as I watered rosebushes, piñon trees,
sage, bamboo, evergreens,
lilacs, saber cactus,
      the roots of plants in my garden
      grip the earth below my bare feet
      into brown fist
    wrenching from the darkness
    what they need
    and converting into beauty,
and I've done that, in a mad near-death dance,
demanding with thundering silence in my eyes
that the dry lightning of light and
    sweet twilight rain
    come from my dreams and yearnings and become substance
    that is as limber and green and colorful
      quiet, strong and humble
    in my life.

It must be so.
>   I've secluded myself for four years
>   in the rock pit called the heart
>   as the rock-crusher days smashed the walls,
>   I veered and ducked, bobbed and weaved
>   from the razor-sharp flying granite chips
that sometimes cut my cheeks, brow and chest,
memories
>   imbedded in my flesh,
>   my body integrates stone in my blood,
>   stone in my soul,
>   stone in my heart.

What I am saying
is that my garden reflects our love, sweet Lisana,
it defines who I am,
it describes my journey
>   in its seasonal succulence
>   of grief and joy,
it remains, offering its bounty as it closes the circle
from bare stems and thorned boughs,
>   presents itself to me
>   as I clamber out of bed.
>   and go outside,
>   I feel the world like an empty opera house
>   and each shrub plant and flower
>   arcs its ragged head and opens its woody mouth
>   to sing in silence of my journey.
>   I look down at each plant
>   as if I were a boy again in the evening,
>   gazing down at a well of my life
>   filled with pure black water
>   its surface glinting with stars
sparkling
>   in the darkness—
in the woods
my life is a harpsichord I hear playing at a distance

and the musician
makes me feel more alone than ever
and yet connected to the universe.

Two

When you are angry, Lisana,
the house becomes a cold cellar.
And each room is filled with echoes.
Echoes of people needing help.
       Your anger is not a clear flame, but I think of those
            fires
       lit by tramps in doorways to keep their toes and
            fingers warm,
       a smoldering black fire kindled with wet bark,
       the smoke warming them
       more than anything else.
Smoke comes from you.
You are not brittle and dried but soft and sensuous,
       limber twigs of anger
       one can bend and twine the bark,
       your emotions
           stripped
              peeled
                 do not burn but smoke,
                   turning your face ashen,
your words lost in the fog,
in our dark coats of skin, our heads down,
we pass each other,
    cold strangers to each other.

              *   *   *

Your face at the door exiled me
from your heart

ugly scene at the car
two of us yelling
raging we would leave and never see each other
again.

How many times I fail
how many times I have dragged myself in at
dawn
and yet I have these words to tell how I love you
I am incompetent at love
I scuttle-slide on clawed rage around on sand
and in my skulled heart
I chew the carcass of guilt I drag behind me
dead thing of guilt
culled from compost heap of decaying life
maggots eels scorpions black widows worms
are the best I have to offer sometimes—
the sweet fragrant apple orchards I promised
you, our first love
we descended in
cool underground cellar where fruit was
gunnysacked
rich black earth I promised we'd plant our seeds
in—
this compost heap is who I am, simmering dead roughage and
gnawed fruit cores—
but I refuse to despair
and in the truck I feel my sadness all over me,
driving, I sing
about how I'm going to make it,
yes I will
about how I'm going to make it,
going to step right in my suffering,
a man slipping on ice,
going to step right in my suffering
going to do it

yes I am
and I shake my sound coming from my mouth to stretch and ease
    and thickly cover my
dark feeling
                I pour my sound from my mouth over my feeling
                    blue
                that I've failed everyone
including myself and I sing
                how I've destroyed myself,
just destroyed myself
                grunt-war-boom-blast of sound
because I'm not going to go down and die
                I said I'm not going to lie down and die
                I'm not going to do it, woman,
                I love you
don't show it
don't have it
don't know how to
never learned to receive it
never knew what it feels like
                but I'm going to have it
                going to have it
I can't live without it, without it, you know.

                There are no reference points to guide me from
                    dissolution to
health
                God, how I would love to be healthy
                pure-bodied crisp-hearted musical-muscled
                    intoning my chorus
love of life
                with each step
                but I live in green prisons of emotions
what I love entraps me in glowing ardor of earthen whimpering
the ivy, the ground, the fires, the sky, the friendships
                all drunkenly charted in destructive courses

over bloody seas of all-night talks
                    but when fathers are with their children on the
                        couch reading fairy tales
I am in deep-bone fever
                    trying to tongue-curl in the minutes of each hour
                    white flakes melting on my tongue
tasting cold life, the cold winter world
                    I balk at domestic scenes and love them
                    I want to stop drinking and love drinking
                    I want to love you forever, my woman,
and I wish to never see you again
                    I want to stay here and I also wish to be alone on
                        a mountain-goat trail
overlooking a vast strange city of lights at night
                    not under this lamp at my desk
but my cheek to the sea waves, a black sailor's coat, gloves and
        cap on.
I love poetry and hate it
I desire what I cannot have, I love my drinking friends and detest them
                    I am a man making love with life
                    but she is no longer beautiful, she is crippled,
                      feet twisted
wearing a full-length leg brace my fingers caress silver straps and
        hitches.
                    Life—this broken bitch who loves me so much
                    reads my palms and howls at my contradictions
                    flips over cards and shows me the hangman
                      sneering at me
shows me pictures of her and me as teenagers dating
                    on the front lawn in perfect bodies, tight shorts,
                    breast cleaved
hair and eye a luxury of love to feel and lose oneself in
                    now grayed with bitterness and gypsy-joker
                    foolish fantasy.

                    Life, how once she was vigorous and
                      brimming—face, hands, legs, thighs

laughter and silence lifted me up into flight
 I knew what the bird felt
and now

 she molds on a bed, unable to get up, disfigured,
 telling me stories
of her imprisonment
 how her love
 abandoned her
 how after she mourned my cold heart
she gave herself to any passerby
 in any park or strange apartment
wishing to dissolve, cut away that part of herself that was me
 dawn rose bloody ax dripping with our wounds
and now after so long I turn and see her everywhere, on crutches,
 smoking cigarette butts
applying stale perfume to her wrist and earlobes
 and it was not supposed to be like this
 not her lying in a cheap cotton blanket
shedding hair
 not her lying on a bed dreaming I will come
degrade myself with her again
 denigrate my gift, shifting her prone lifeless body
 under me so I can
fuck her in ten minutes and leave with my head down, shamed
 and violated
 my spirit seed having saved itself
 impregnated my emptiness with infection of
 cruelty I spread in others.

✳   ✳   ✳

You buy a bottle and life is better?
You snap your fingers and she rises to you?
Your teeth scummed with bread shared with thieves and liars
you spend time with men crucified to their egos, willfully
 spitting at morality
 blood-sucking swamp-mouthed vipers
 I tolerate

I know deep in my heart
are anti-life
whose hair is matted with death juices . . .

Life is deeply moving to me.
I will become healthy, I will
survive and live a balanced life,
full of real feelings unvarnished by whiskey
I'll necklace my original beauty
and break the crust of arrogant years with
            humble light.

I want to call someone to me now to hold me
            I am tired of the shove, brusque slug, elbow-
                  ribbing or backslap
our relationship keeps itself apart
            because of me
            how I am unable to let myself be human
What am I to say, in sad wonder and revelation,
of the man in me accumulating life
            rusty wrecks of bomb-shelled iron
            of the man in me handshaking ambassadors and
                  university presidents
who foul-mouth the common spirit
            and of the man who overcomes adversity
            and of the man so weak and futile goddamned
                  fucked up
            I can't see my way out anymore
I lay wounded in the frontline trench, slowly bleeding to death
as life all around reduces itself to screams of terror
            of men who never did what they could have done
            of women who assault their dignity with abusive men
self-deprecating, decorated with lies
            honored and despised
            helpless and healing
            strong and forward, fertile with primal knowledge
            up at dawn and by evening stumble-mouthed idiots

afraid and yet fearless, pompous and pious, loving and lost,
wanting someone to hold.

Beyond all the drivel and doggerel yap-heap
the sore-souled lip-bitten held-too-long silence
beyond the neglect scorn abuse
I need to be touched and held
as preposterous as a man with asthma jogging while puffing a
cigarette
I think of myself
and yet when I turn the light off and see how the
full moon
shines and glimmers on the brown leaves in the yard
the light
brings me so much quiet joy
and I can live.

We keep pulling each other into
our nets
our cages
our locked rooms
our sickness
gobs in our lungs we cannot pull out
affects the way we breathe and feel
voodoo iguanas in our stomachs
make us snarl and cough
make us other than we are
entangle us
against each other we pull at the hair feeling the pain
we pull at the tail feeling the pain.
And yet our relationship
glistens with wet sparkling dew-melt
your laughter
burns proudly roadside peaks with white tip-voice looming into
the crystalline sky
our relationship is snowmelt
melting down into a thousand winding creeks

and there is the avid green pine-needle fragrance in our words
the wet-give mulch underfoot of forgiveness
                and another level of survival together
                we do not give up
                we will not give up
                we will not stop dreaming
                and we are learning to scream
with a raised fist and in the other hand our hearts offered
                and we are learning to take the heart.

I start—
                climb my heart
                in the manner a rock climber starts to a distant peak.
                From that point I can see farther into my feelings
                curl up by the stars
taking no map with me, route my making
                on instinct, truth, faith
                no books, ropes, boots, jackets, store foods
                bare-chested in my own wild terrain
                light a fire
                with what I find along the way
learning how to live again
                with who I am.

Three

Something happened
as if in the daily goings-on of my life,
        while packing boxes to move away, while washing clothes,
        angels assembled in the red cathedral of my heart
        and they sang a certain unique song
        that peeled from my eyes an old wax paper that made what
                I viewed
                        much clearer,

It was as if
carrying my murdered father, mother and brother in my soul,
    what should have been black bread and vinegar for my meal,
    suddenly, I was looking at each one and bidding them
        good-bye
    with glass after glass of Russian vodka,
and the rain that afternoon poured upon me while running on the
    West Mesa
    a thousand violins and trumpets shook the skies and
        vibrated in my bones
and no matter where I've gone since then,
    to the coffee shops, theater, grocery store,
    each building and street and anonymous face presents itself
    with a refreshed welcome.
I rise for no reason in the middle of the night,
my body limber as a dancer's, muscled and sleek,
    thinner than I was before my grief, less apt to indulge in the
        miracle of movement,
    now I move like a swan at night across the glistening black
        water of silence
        room to room,
        as if I were a long drawn-out solitary cello note filling
            each room
        with my own song of remorse and grief,
the grief slowly rising into a somber celebration of survival, into a
    brown, honey-sweet song
that I have come to through the spiked clutches of bereavement.
        I move on now,
        I move on from the embrace you gave me in the
            bedroom promising to be mine,
that you were only going home for a visit and would remain my
    true love,
you were giving me time to clear my things,
to finish up the book, finish up the script, and you promised
            our love would remain intact,
            that since I was busy, a brief visit to your parents
            to see how your father was

would be good while I finished my writing projects,
but you lied—
and then as I finished the book, the dead rose from graves to
        grab at me,
pleading for me not to release them.
                But I moved on,
                        releasing you as I released the dead,
        at first blinded by the pitch-black tunnel I found myself
wandering in,
        blinded by the vodka, by my own convulsive grief,
                I even turned my back on the sunrise,
                deaf to God, blind to light, I wanted no one around me.
                        All the promises I had believed in,
that my life would be filled with your love, Lisana,
the promise that cometed from your mouth red-hot to wait for
        me, to go only for a visit,
                        split into knife blades, sharp slivers under my
                                tongue, imbedded
themselves in my bare feet,
                        pierced my eyes, pinched my fingers until they
                                were purple,
                        and the blessings I had hoped for turned into
                                condemnations,
                        the hope I counted on turned into hopelessness,
                        the love I waited for emptied gravel into my
                                heart and weighed it down
                until like an anchor it pulled me down to the deepest
                depths of each day
where I drowned,
                a sailor's corpse tossed from his boat crushed by a
                        storm,
                I dangled without breath or life in the sea of sadness,
                        at the mercy of each wave.

                    *   *   *

Somehow I awake this morning as if hurled onto a strange and
        wonderful beach,

I stand and look around, finding myself on this strange island
　　called my life.
　　　　　I have so much to celebrate, so much to tell you,
　　　　　exhorting you to spread your wings and fly,
let not the lie rule the day,
let not deception turn our tongues to wood
　　　　　let not a loveless life make us straw men and women
　　　　　　　stuffed with forage
　　for beasts to fill their guts on.
　　　　　　　　I now align
　　　　　　　myself with the flowers in the garden,
　　I now take as my weapon against the darkness of loneliness
　　my own heart in hand like a lantern a boy holds on the dark
　　　　road
　　　　　that leads home.

I was told by a friend that after the roses bloomed, if I cut off the
　　old bud
new roses would bloom,
　　and I waited, every day checking them, watering them,
　　　　talking to them,
　　　　　　until this morning I go outside to water them
　　　　　　　　and during the night the pink, red, white
　　　　　　　　　and faded roses
　　　　　　　　　all arrived like happy pilgrims
　　　　　　　　　　exiled from home
　　　　　　　　　　　　disembarking a train and
　　　　　　　　　　　　　crowding
　　　　　　　　　　the garden beds
　　　　　　　　　　　with their
　　　　　　　　　　　　　clamor and
　　　　　　　　　　　fragrance and joy.
That is the way we are, first blooming beautiful,
　　　　　　then snipped,
　　　　　　　then blooming again.
　　　　I am discovering magic in me again, Lisana, I
　　　　have no fear of packed

boxes

        as I used to, so often as a child when I was happy
and came back to where I was living

          I'd find a box of my belongings packed and I'd
            be moved again,

      not now—

          and even more, in the midst of facing all I
            fear,

          I feared saying good-bye to my murdered
            parents and brother,

but I did,

          I feared you leaving me, but you did, and I
            bowed in your

direction.

      My heart brimming over with love for you,
      I pray every day for you,

          pray that you follow your soul and continue
            dance classes

          pray that you make love with a spiritual essence
you must call forth from your being,

          you must use it to heal, to make your life,

          as your soul longs for the lightning that yoga and
            low-fat diets cannot

satiate,

          you've forgotten that

          your beauty resides in your honesty, in your
            beauty of heart, in your

sweetness of soul,

          so my adorable Lisana, take to the dawn as if you
            were a flower

          and second-bloom your soul, second-bloom your
            heart,

          let your smile radiate to the ends of the earth,
            welcome the water and fire and earth and sky
            and I will sit here, carving a talisman of my
              heart, a red wooden

figurine
                    doing my prairie voodoo prayers to keep you
                              safe, to keep you cherished,
that no harm come your way,
                    that blessings sprinkle on the ground where you
                              set your footsteps
                    as you take your journey onward,
                              blessed are you,
                              loved are you,
                                        my sweet Lisana.

Four

I go running by myself in the trashlands
on the West Mesa by the dormant volcanoes,
                    dusty roadside littered
                              with tires, Styrofoam, beer bottles, crushed
                              headlights, broken
TVs, plumbing pipes, mounds of roofing squares and gravel and
     tar splats,
black plastic trash bags, McDonald's soda cups,
                    and still up pops a big-eared jackrabbit, scampering
                              with quick zigzag hops through brush,
and I'm pleased,
                    around rubber mats, used lumber piles, rusting pipes
                              and fencing,
                    remembering how
not to deceive myself with false friends, but to grow as the sky
     grows blue,
let myself expand universally over the earth with goodwill and love,
     to change voraciously, travel, meet new friends, go places,
     and I am learning to write from six-thirty to
          eight-thirty A.M., then go

to a coffee shop, enjoy myself,
do not avoid confronting my dreams and hopes,
let them
meet me like the rattlesnake I met yesterday on
the dirt road,
its designs of bracelets and necklaces in the dust
sensuously curved across the dirt,
risk failure,
allow rejection in my life, if certain people
must avoid me, let them,
never tolerate inappropriate situations,
get rid of those who bring negative energy
into my home,
never tolerate lies, deceptions,
and I thank you as I run up the winding roads, sniffing the wind
that is like a sunbonneted aproned woman
bending in the sage fields picking up
fragrances
as if she were in the market picking up the
morning's fruit.
I remind myself to accept my emotions,
like a bird catching an updraft and fighting with furious
wings beating to steady itself
on the air, I do, I am always choosing to change for the better, to
confront, to leap into the wind,
to be
as fully filled with my inherent love and beauty, always
pouring out from
my fingertips,
to be available to love,
until I become the hummingbird I was once, trusting
to land in the open
palm,
praying I do not get crushed,
always affirming my freedom to love and be
loved—
sweating, exhausted, I shower now,

                              scrub down my body with soap
                    and water,
                    breathing,
                    glistening,
                    transforming into a fish,
                    a scaled winged serpent blue and red
                              and turquoise,
                    I thrash from the water and fly
                              toward love this

morning,

              through the green leaves of dawn light,
                    I fly.

Five

I have these obsessions of the heart.
Losing you, Lisana, I think of an image:
a hummingbird's beak
grown old and cracked,
searching for nectar in the stone flowers of your heart.
        I remember
how our love once had green and red feathers
flitting and suspended, up and down
in its love dance.
        How
did our love become the hummingbird
trapped in the chimney fireplace,
buried in stove ash, beating itself
against the stove glass, trying to free myself?

I swing open the stove door
take it in my hand and go out the front door and release it.
        I feel the hummingbird's heart
beating with fright in my palm,

feel its wings and bones and beak
flit freely into the moonless night.
and my tears are the first drops of nectar on its beak.

*   *   *

My mind starts to forget the special moments,
	I find myself comparing
myself to others
	healthier than I,
who never smoked or did drugs or stayed awake for days
routinely—I even imagine
what I might look like in a coffin,
	whether there'll be anyone there to mourn me,
	will my color be right, the collar on the stain pillow
	starched and pressed,
	there'll be no need then to wonder about evenings
	we had, Lisana, when we loved and quarreled,
staying at the apartment you were house-sitting,
being with you that cold December week,
dreams came to me like a guitar playing in a dark alley,
the notes soft as a nurse's hands rubbing my sore muscles.

In another dream, I'm lying in bed
watching lovers, when the meaning of happiness
comes with clarity, and the guitar notes are sad,
when in the dream the woman you love
		gets up beside you
		and leaves,
		when the evil of lust
		promises
		you happiness
and instead has you walking alone in the cemetery,
under the leafless branches,
wondering why the previous night we went out to eat
we got drunk and later at the apartment
you left me asleep in bed
and went driving around the city,

the snow piled six inches in the street,
banked up on the sides as snowplows
trucked through the sparkling dark,
and you gripping the steering wheel, gloved, capped,
coated, breathing fog on the windows,
numb with sorrow, weeping
      to understand the snow, what love is,
      how the snow that moment surrounded you with its chill
          love,
      its pure white prayer for refuge,
      reflecting a silence you absorbed.

While driving me later
      to the airport,
you told me you had made love to other men
while we were apart,
and I knew in my silence it would take time
to heal the wound, the fear,
        to trust you again.
I went up the elevator stairs
to a plane toward home, without looking back,
my heart buried beneath the snow and ice,
      it cracked under the asphalt
      with frozen palpitations
      wandering in all directions,
seeking love, a place to break free through the ice,
but there was nothing, only your cold pale face
above the ice.

The streetlamp glows dimly
      in the empty parking lot,
      its orb of light
      reflected off the crystalline snow, our silence
when you drove me to the airport—
      a few businessmen in trench coats, scarves and gloves
      track across the snow toward empty buildings,
      lulled into a dead sleep by the snowstorm.

Six

Lisana, what an unbelievable week
　　　　　starting Sunday when talking with you
hurt me so much,
needing you and loving you and wanting you and seeing you with me
accompanying me
being with me
　　　seeing you see yourself with me
in my house in Taos,
　　　leading your own life, empowering yourself
　　　with your own talents and efforts
　　　and my love—
　　　　　　I heard myself put questions to you—
do you want a man to stand at your side,
someone you can trust,
who will never betray you or abandon you,
someone in the morning
　　　whom you look at and feel love for, someone
all sweet, a sweet heart, sweet body, sweet smile, sweet words,
who will stand at your side through health or sickness
　　　and yet
　　　permits you to go where you must to feed your soul,
but never, never, Lisana, give up your heart to another,
　　　when once we ritualize our love.
Never allow anyone to violate our trust again,
not me or you,
we commit ourselves to each other in our souls
and hearts
　　　and make our affection and love and respect and trust
sacred.

*   *   *

Imagine our hearts to be beautiful pianos in a room
and we vow to let only our love play the pianos,
when we are in New York
play for me, love,
when we are in Taos on our farm, I'll play for you, my love,
I'll cuddle and nourish and care for you and empower your struggle
with my belief and faith in you.
    All this went through my mind
as I drank vodka and smoked cigarettes, staring at the sky and
        groaning
quietly to myself
all night,
hurting for you,
not wanting to cry but feeling like crying,
not wanting you in my life
but loving you to be in my life—
    That morning after talking with you,
I went up to the mesa and ran my heart out, I ran faster and
        longer than I ever did
because I thought I was going to die if I didn't run, I had to run,
        breathe, pray,
And while running, up to the volcano, through cactus, through
        grass,
I started weeping,
    and it all started falling into place.

Strange things started happening—
the urge to drink to ease the pain to numb the hurt of your
        leaving me
was absent, gone completely.
I was wandering in my life again
at the beginning before I knew you, starting anew,
wandering in a land full of potential and possibilities.

    I felt no jealousy,
    if you must then go with my blessings,

La Guerra   157

travel the world, see people, love them,
wander to your heart's contentment,
be who you must be,
pursue your dreams without me.

            But I must tell you
how I dream of you every night,
waking up Tuesday, Wednesday, Thursday, Friday, Saturday
        at five-thirty with a renewed vigor and clarity in my life.

I run at dawn, huffing hard but with certainty
that something deep in me is changed.
        The hawk following me, a rattlesnake
        coiled tight as a faded gray silver dollar
        in the path, a tarantula hurrying over a rock,
        and I feel all creation coursing in my blood
        throbbing like a flamenco dancer
pounding heels on the wooden stage of my soul exhorting me
with her feverish beat and hot-blooded cries and clappings of
        castanets—

Jimmy, dance with the world! Adelante *Santiago! Dance, my love!*
            And every day passes with thoughts of you like yellow
                butterflies
flitting beneath my flesh,
        I see me sleeping next to you, devoted to you, loving you,
            kissing your sweet body,
        o, I see myself being the man you hike with,
        at dawn walking, breakfasting in cafés,
        laughing and hugging
this man I am
is a jazz song on a baritone sax
        a deep bass humming low buzzing of love,
            until your eyes weep with faith that I love you, Lisana.

        And so much else happened,
all week I wanted to write you,

me trucking load after load of stuff from the house to
    storage,
no longer afraid of the future, no longer alien to myself.
I smile
    and people smile back, I am alone in the world,
    here in the house alone, in the world alone, in my heart
        alone.
    And my voice, while still mellow, is strong and completely
        whole,
is my voice again
and my wicker-basket heart carries overflowing roses and lilies I
    give with each breath to the
world around me.
Here in the living room I wade through flowers,
with every breath flowers come out and I cover the sidewalks
    with flowers,
flowers flying out of my truck window.

    Lisana, I love your loving me, I love your giving me your
        love,
I love your weeping in my arms, trusting me, laughing the way
    you do
as if scores of dolphins broke the surface water at night and
    sparkled silver moons
silver laughing waves all around them,
my sweet porpoise,
    arching your body, I dream you next to me, both of us
        following a wandering creek that is our road together,
        now that my life has humbled itself like autumn leaves
            blowing
across the lake,
now that my hours are silent and I meditate on how much your love
    meant to me
how much you mean to me
how much I know we were meant to be together,
    it all humbles me and I lower my head and ask your forgiveness

for hurting you,
vowing it will never happen again.

Now that I have dealt with my grief,
now that I have survived my own nightmares,
I don't worry whether you're ever going to be with me,
nor do I worry about why you don't spread your arms to
everyone
and announce your love to me,
I don't worry that you won't be on the farm with me,
or to start our School of Healing Dance.

It matters little
how you toddle and postpone your commitment to me,
or if you go to Latin America or Mexico
and love a different man every night,
it matters nothing to me anymore because I love you
the way I turn up the volume on a good song and it fills the
whole house
with sunshine streaming in every window,
all that matters
is truth,
and I send you mine, filled with love
and positive glowing radiant energy,
I send you unmitigated love for giving me the gift of your
precious love.

Listen, love, listen to my snapping fingers keep beat with
the sweet jazz of your love,
o, it's sweet,
snap them fingers, brother, snap them fingers, sister,
tap your shoes, nod your head to Lisana's sweet jazzy love,
listen to her heart blow that trumpet up bee-bop-do-wop,
whirling notes from her hips and legs and back and lips and
chirping like
a bird gone mad on spring fragrance.

O Lisana, I love you, sweet hot mama,
        and yet the magic keeps coming day after night,
until alone as usual, thinking of you, I pull out the manuscript
and, sitting outside in the garden by myself,
        I start reading passages aloud,
            when suddenly a prairie dove flies over the wall.

        It beats its wings to get in my living room window,
            it calms down and gently lands a foot from me as I read
and I have the strongest premonition it is a spirit
wishing me well, protecting me, blessing me,
        and I stare at the prairie dove, it doesn't move, it isn't
            afraid, it just
                stares at me with a peaceful expression almost
                    filled with love and
empathy
            I sense an undeniable and familiar recognition
                between us,
making the pain of missing you almost bearable,
    making the mistakes I made with you
clearly ones that I would never make again—
        but it's over.

        And now I rise early and bicycle the river, climb the mountain,
follow the river, travel to a wonderful city, become a quiet man,
filled with dignified reserve.
        I travel to Europe, Africa, Mexico, Ireland, England,
remembering you at the dance workshop in San Diego,
your healing dance made your dreams
flesh out, grow teeth, hair, arms and hands and legs.

I remember how you wept in my arms every time after we had sex,
after orgasm, after hurt, after dancing,
I remember how you clung to me, needed me passionately,
and you never knew how when you left
        you didn't see me

on that balcony in Los Angeles every night writing you love poems,
at the airport on the floor with my laptop writing you love poems—
	you'll never have a love like mine, Lisana, ever.

	I rode my '49 Harley up to the Sandia Peak, and it was so
		beautiful,
the quiet beauty of tall pines and green grass and oak and dogwood,
the engine vibrating, the wind hugging me,
the pines kissing me, my coat collar turned up,
feeling good by myself, thinking of times
we made love in the roadside weeds and grass,
snuggled, filled with warm affection—
		I have so much love to give,
so many poems to write,
so many places I want to visit,
so many experiences I want to share,
			because love
is the sweetest of minerals to bathe myself in,
wing myself with,
claw myself in,
let it consume me in its passionate hungering . . .

			✳ ✳ ✳

Ah, but I have the same disease that most men have—
loving a woman who's gone.
I blame the light in her
		for my obsession of the heart:
attracted by the light cupping her breasts,
by the whip-crack light that snaps
			around her waist,
making me growl like a lion in a circus ring
forced to sit in a chair.
It's the light that springs from her hands
like a delicious plate of Mexican food,
and not allowed to make love to her,
I live like a prisoner in a cell on bread and water rations.
On those occasions,

when her tongue curls into my mouth,
I am the man travelers find in the desert,
a beautiful woman lays me in her arms,
and from a leather water pouch,
        drips cold pure water into my parched mouth.
        Even the light that scorches the desert
        becomes a mere oasis of light
                in her presence.
A light in her attracts me,
not dissuading me from leaving
and moving on with my own life
        but a light that never lets me forget
                                        her:
the fly buzzing against the sun-warmed
        windowpane is me,
the snake absorbing the waves of emanating rock-warmth
        is me,
the lilac bud tightly encased in its green scales
        barely starting to unfurl in the winter light
        when freezing night cold makes it draw back
        is me.

Seven

I write to you out of a deep loneliness and solitude
of one, a Chicano, who would love to listen tonight to Chicano
        spiritual drums
        to laughter roughly at my window screen
                and *la gente* with torches glowing with deeper meaning
than I have tonight.
        We need rituals to heal us,
        passages from sorrow into joy. We
        who have taken thousands of journeys into grief need one
                Chicano, Chicana

to march along the ditch bank tonight and sing to the flowers
make our mouth a moon
we need one symbol, then another
to bring us back to our spirit as a *gente.*

I have cursed Christ,
blamed St. Francis and St. Anthony for my wretched life, accused
     them
of conspiracy to shovel heaps of our souls into coal piles
              behind prisons
              behind hospitals.
I have turned my back on heaven because it pressed on me
with nightmares—not dreams
with damnation—not salvation
with curses—not blessings.
I turned on Christ with glassy blue lying eyes,
with teeth-biting lips
and bone-chill loneliness.
I screamed at Christ, *You belong to them!*
How I hurt!
My soul filled with green bile of rage.
I turned against everyone, so young.

I felt myself apart from the world—those terrible afternoons
when kids were in school and old people sat at windows sewing
     work pants,
I was the only kid in the world, all the men at work, kids in
     classrooms,
I felt as apart as a young strong arm lopped off from its shoulder,
my invisible hand reaching out holding nothing—
my ears burning with the scorn and poverty I was born into.
My silence was a tribute to the shame that I had no country, no
     culture, no god.
I had been denied access to society, *un niño con corazón lleno, lleno de amor*
     para toda la vida
and crushed
to become an emotional amputee

under God's batons
on God's bloody streets
by God's racist police
(you must remember that right now there are thousands of
    young men and women
being brutally beaten in county jails and prisons)
till my life became a series of numb blazing drunks and
    drugged
stupors
    so as not to feel my self-hate and self-abhorrence
    so as not to feel my own bleeding.

I want to ask forgiveness tonight. You are a public witness. I ask
    blessing from
four directions. I greet the sun blowing a kiss on my hand upward.
        This is a letter of forgiveness
        to myself
        and I do not know why I say that.
        I am so tired of rejecting the Creator,
        the saints, Jesus, the earth
        in all I do and have done
        in my Chicano rage and pride.
A man in me has learned to create light in self-created darkness only.
He ignores the light in books, in friends, in the dawn,
and burns in the dark—
        what a futile fool I have been!
        I do not say this to the perfect ones,
        not for them
        do I forgive myself in God's eyes
        but before my fellow human beings, brothers and sisters
        all those millions of people
        struggling for dignity and fulfillment
        do I ask forgiveness
        for giving up the hope to know my true face and speak my
            true heart,
        please forgive me.

                    *   *   *

I waited too long thinking the judge would solve injustice
too long I waited for the mail to announce me acceptable
too long I waited and became old and bitter waiting
        and I know this night I trust myself again
        and believe in the words I write
        I have moved the rock pile my heart is into a circle
        and thrown everything I believe
        in the middle
        and these words I light in the center of the circle
        and dance around the fire tonight
        for these words
        are as truthful as I can make myself write.

        I will not seal off the light,
        eclipse the moon in my eyes
        and let darkness settle between us anymore.

I dance the ritual dance of a death—
there are two men in me and one must die.
The warrior has forgotten which way the temple is,
he forgot the ancestral path,
how to celebrate the light and give humble praise to Quetzalcoatl
        in too many bottles of whiskey, in too many arguments
        in too many sleepless nights of cocaine
        in too many thoughts of just I
        I know it
        I will fight
        I will grieve
        I I I
damned be I, I sing! Sing
        that I'm only a flower's opening gasp
        and then wintry silence.

        A Chicano boy in me tonight
        kneels at the altar in a small mountain chapel
        and prays all the world into his soul
        who needs food should have it

who is drunk should sober
who is homeless should have shelter
who rages should have peace
the little boy has all the saints, Gods, prophets, priests, nuns, monks
rituals, symbols of creative healing with him
    but somewhere along a Chicano warrior grew in him/me
    the Gregorian chants on the boy's lips
    dulled on the warrior's mouth who pursed his lips as police
        beat him
    the flurry of joyous voices in the choir the boy sang in
    snarled into gang-fight cries of hurt and rage
    and the soft music of birds at dawn
    slurred into drunken brawls of men at bars
    and the roses he so loved to smell and touch
    became bruises on his own body he hated to touch and see
    the jingle of pocket change his grandfather gave him for
        candy
    became hostile clicking of keys in cell doors
    the glimmering jeweled chalice the priest raised at mass
    turned to glimmering whiskey bottles and police headlights
        at night
    and glinting switchblades
    the gleam of dewdrops on windows at dawn
    dried to crusty streaks on his cheeks
    the warrior's callused palm wiped each tear away.

It all seems so clear to me tonight.
The warrior rose in me as the resurrection of a corpse from
    a grave
how nobody I was how nothing I was how I would be
    nobody
how there was nothing in this society for me
except the sad autumn afternoon and its overwhelming
    loneliness
every bottle of whiskey tried to quench
every lie tried to invent me
every court tried to subject me

every school tried to shame me
every job tried to enslave me
every map tried to reroute me
every book tried to describe me
but the warrior spat in disgust at the boy's naïveté, the warrior
ran out of things to hate
and I no longer believe in the warrior
but in the boy's hunger and yearning for symbols to heal
for rituals to celebrate the warrior's death,
that he be buried with dignity and ceremony.
What the warrior touched he wrecked and butchered
in blind maddening hurt
he drained life in his own unyielding need to create a life
wild with renegade sessions of drinking and fighting and
lawless disorder
was his solitary expression of grief
was his feverish fear that life was too hard any other way
that it hurt too much, there was too much pain
afraid he would be mauled and cannibalized
he shielded himself.

And now, tonight, I feel remorse and sadness for him
I kneel at the little church at Isleta
in front of *La Virgen de Guadalupe*
and weep out my sins, pray that she forgives me
pray for all warriors on the streets with so much talent and
genius
that goes unexpressed and they slowly die
I commit myself to prayer, contemplation, and ask forgiveness.
I am a tired bull who has come to the foothills of the city
asking the boy to pull the swords and lances from my heart.

Nothing else applies but silence, meditation, courage and love
let the war words rust, cease clique battles
admit I don't know the way
I am creeping in the dark unable to reach the light switch
but with reserve and humility

I'll listen for my ancestors humming in my heart
old rituals for healing
I'll descend to the core of darkness and retrieve the bone-flower
    images
    that will have men dancing again
    praising life, praising family, praising heartbeat.
With symbols and rituals for healing
we will again hold our ears to the heartbeat . . .
    it's been so long since I have listened to yours
    I kneel and ask forgiveness from all people
    whose hearts I have ceased to listen to in many years . . .
        forgive me!

Eight

Breaking up
    is not like a Hollywood film, no rainy
dark streets, no winds gusting at trees or leaves
booming branches against wooden picket fences.
    There's the city in its awesome
warring metal and rock and glass, so
structured the weak are stepped on,
driven to live in despair and labor.
    But to love in such a city? To reach out
to another person and love that person through a crisis,
wade knee-deep through doubt and fear,
through your own cracked segments of life,
your life falling about you in grand upheaval,
to crunch your own cataclysmic epoch

                                    and reach,

    reach for someone to love,
    be loyal through the parading debris
    flung up at you in gay illusions,
    to find yourself among crowds and confusion,

locate that strand and fiery fiber
that shocks your sense, rusty and coiled,
into fierce and raging locomotion,
spewing fire out your heart
for the one you love, you love.

Our passions are the fiery altars
where we sacrifice the sweet gold of Reason,
altars where we learn to believe
in superior beings above,
for when in love, one can look around and see no longer
the straight line, instead all is crooked and craned
and stressing to burst out like spring flowers
where soldiers fall in bloody wounds and cannons roar
and church bells mourn and sing their lonely dirges,
when in love,
words carry that death charge glowing
in our breast, words burn their light
through dark halls in our soul,
words spoken by our lover
puff at our dusty story of life,
like an old book slapped open by wind
from the window, and ruffling through yellow pages
reading stories of our life.

A man and a woman create a circle when they are in love,
breaking the circle, one leaves out to utter black space,
the other slowly watching the energy dim,
crumbling, and the circle like a disc
swirls maddeningly through space, an outer-space craft
that will, when it lands, leave gaping craters smoldering
in green grass. Those craters are the footsteps
                                        of lovers apart.

Nine

I am trying to say
if you want to be with me, be with me,
      if you don't, then don't—
if the latter is true, don't let these poems flatter you,
    they are intended for more than flattery,
        they are birth poems of love from me to you,
        from my abdomen, full of blood, fear, love, guilt,
            devotion.
Do not love me, do not commit yourself to me, do not honor me
with your heart
        if you secretly don't intend to, if you don't want to.
I must move on, to fall in love with trees, cathedral bells, soft
    evenings, snowy mountains,
cafés, books, music.
        Start your life,
        create your environment where you flourish, where
            your gifts
become fire to the kindling in drought-stricken souls,
become the woman you desire.

What good is love if you desire another between us,
what good is love if you flirt with others,
what good is love if you do not surrender yourself to your lover
as I would to you, fully and totally, with complete honesty and
    commitment,
        your knees, your breast, your lips, your voice,
      the only reason I love them is because of the soul-energy
        that fills them.
Your heart and soul

are like the rarest of turquoise jungle birds,
fit only for warrior hearts,
        which I have, which I live with and which I offer you.

Tonight I wish I could dine with you, candlelight and wine,
low talk, listening to you tell me things, teach me of your soul
        and dreams,
tonight I wish I could go to a movie and hold your hand,
whisper my thoughts to you.
Tonight we could walk, we could drive to the mountaintop and
        tell each other
our fondest wishes and most coveted dreams,
        and what you shared with me I would cherish,
        hold close to my heart like a young boy with a flame in each
                hand
to lead him through the dark.

You must understand, leave or stay, but know
                I believe and have tremendous faith
        that if you flung fear away, if you truly loved me, you'd tell
                the world
                of your love, conceal nothing,
                        and I would in turn do the same.
I would never let you down.

Tonight it is late and I'm alone again,
        I see you in New York stepping out of a cab,
        I see you camping in the mountains and telling me your
                feelings,
        I see your heart
                when I look at the moon,
        I see your smile when I see the hummingbird at the lilac
                bush,
        I see your soul
                when I inhale the air
                that allows me to live,

I feel you in me,
feel myself in you,
feel the throbbing, the panting, the crying
the embrace
so tight
I see you walking down black steps in a white skirt.

I see you in a gallery holding a brochure, viewing
    paintings,
I see you studying the woman's face in a painting
    I see a man flirt with you
I see you flirt back
I see you go with a man in a bar
I see you desiring another man
    and I see myself vanish into the smoky steam of
        a dark street
    never to return.
I lose myself in a bookstore,
I lose myself in a busy street lined with jazz clubs,
    in a studio recording poetry with musicians in
        New Orleans
    but vanishing from your life
        the way a dormant volcano awakens with
            red roaring
    to love fully
coagulating into black lava rock that will remain like scabs
    covering the green grass that could
have been
beneath its black sharp scales of hardened lava crust.

There is no jealousy in me, just a need for truth,
    as I meditate on life more and more,
        I need truth,
and I need love, lasting love.

Ten

There is nothing more unbelievable than the world
we live in,
considering that each man has something unidentified
and each woman some miraculous mist
                                        in their hearts.
When woman is raveled in sheets,
I observe her in the even softer meaty folds
of my mind, she rages with acute sensuality.
        There is a special woman.
The more I see of her, the less beautiful she becomes.
Time has tarnished the glow, dizzied the clear perception of her,
and in each withering day that passes,
there is a frantic loss stoking dead embers in me,
there is in me the need to find what, why,
things turned out so.
                    So real and unreal,
into a fair and pleasant death one does not attend,
one cannot put the finger on the casket
but hears the weeping deep within, sees the flowers
of gardens take on different shapes and colors.
        There is a woman I have looked for a very long time.
I have carried myself like the sun across each day,
and seldom have I seen her in full beauty,
disappearing into the moon at twilight like a dove.
        But she has become ugly. I remember kissing her legs.
I recall enchanting her with my silliness,
the things I remember!
And time runs out, the one you love leaves,
wind shatters the silence that catches
you alone, as now, wondering what to write to someone,

someone now old, yet young, but old and aged,
whose hair has become coarse, words unpleasant,
whose body declines in strange beds,
whose lips kiss other flesh, whose touch tingles and fires
others, others, others. I'll go my way now.
　　　I know now I know nothing about love, nothing at all.
I spend my life studying love,
it is the great destroyer, teacher and keeper.
I want to know why, what and where of love,
as the most ancient explorer, I go pitting myself,
endangering myself, wandering,
hearing great echoes within me.

Eleven

Later this evening,
alone in a corner of the balcony, in the dark,
with the rumbling of planes overhead, not loud
but humming constantly into LAX,
　　　I see you snuggle deep into the bag,
　　　wish I could breathe into your hands,
face-to-face, smell you,
smell your womanness, your sweat and wildness,
your luxurious heart pounding
　　　　　　the loneliness you say you feel
　　　　　　thinking of me.
Leaning over the balcony this afternoon, taking a break
from writing, I saw an old man and a boy
walking hurriedly on the sidewalk,
the old man carrying a suitcase,
　　　　　then later, after it grew dark,
　　　　　across from me, a woman in a window
　　　　　across the street, in the second story,
　　　sat at her table alone,

then all around me, lives in various stages of living and dying
made me wish we were together,
suckling each minute
germinating our togetherness into abundant banquets
of intimacy,
        humid heavy,
           here with me now,
           instead of so far apart.
We all have lives to live
and the reasons that make us who we are,
the people who influence us, the worries and joys
that become our memories
      set us free, cage us,
      but here I am, listening against this evening to the ocean
      lullaby me in its arms, with stories
           of you and me,
           the hard work we'd experience,
           the waking up, the living each day
               unraveling your life
               in travels and people and places
               me studiously writing another novel, short
                  stories,
poems,
meditating, caring for each other, inwardly
tunneling deeper into each other
until we're so far in
        we sit in a small cave in each other's hearts
        and from there we show each other our lives
        like shells collected on the beach,
like children playing,
sandcastling each other's hearts
and peopling them with kings and queens, horses and fields,
that become us, changing as we will,
        changing healthier, more trusting, loving,
        fusing into one
           huge volcanic love where our words
           take on the magic and reverence

of sweetness of cherries
or apricots glowing gold,
or bear cubs grappling in tall grass
innocent, rough, happy.
So what do I say?
My poems do not replace you,
my poems cannot dissuade you,
my poems are not love that I feel in my body,
they call for you, they need you, they are signs
in the sand
that each pulsing blood wave from my heart
erases sadly, erases sadly, erases,
and I return to the balcony to compose yet another
poem,
wondering if you are just playing me for a fool,
wondering why you don't reach out and take me, wondering why
and what is stopping you
from coming to me.
If it's fear, then keep your fear,
if it's another love, then keep your love and go on in life by
yourself
with your lovers,
I will not mourn you, I'll pray sweet angels
care for you and protect you,
if it's that you don't feel the way I do,
I won't be sad or weep,
I'll ask the powers of earth to guide you,
but now, alone on this balcony, I'm feeling more sad,
more useless with my poetry,
more prepared to go on by myself.
I feel alone but strong,
unloved by you but loved by the ocean,
needing you at my side but okay if I have only myself,
more and more you become the mist, you become
people in windows with each other
you become that woman far away who is not thinking about me
you become a memory

you become someone I cannot trust to love me
as I love you
you become less and less the woman I know and love
more and more a phantom of each evening
        I think about on the balcony
        overlooking the ocean
        thinking perhaps, as I stare at the horizon of endless
            water,
        thinking perhaps I might sail away
alone.
      You see, the whole idea evolves around
        whether you see yourself loving me
        and making a life with me,
    and I'm not crowding you in a corner, I don't care
    to do that, I want you free, but I need commitment
    not immature and characterless indulgence
        that I see so much of here in L.A.
It doesn't have the slightest attraction to me,
not the light and meaningless things either,
like fucking for fucking's sake, like false flattery,
like having a chick because she's got a great body,
my concerns are deeper and more beautiful, more passionate,
more honorable and loving,
      and that's the life I want with you,
        grace with struggle,
      words between us that carry our souls in them
      like flowers with pollen we keep visiting like bees
      or hummingbirds, pollinating the garden of our lives
      with ever new arrangements of beauty.
If you want something else, it's yours.
I'll step aside graciously,
      I seek the magic in life, I want to experience
      what it is to live
        with truth and love,
        I want a true woman to love,
        so that we become wooo-man, one

person, always caring for each other.
The rest you can have.
I'm going to go to bed now and read a book,
light a candle in the dark after I have closed the book.
I gaze at the candle and invent that you're next to me
whispering, holding me, sleeping
wrapped with your legs and arms and face all over me, and I'll
    hug you to me
warmly, nurture you even in your sleep,
so that life you think on waking is a dream
    a beautiful dream with this man
    you call your angel your lover your sweetness.

Twelve

I feel myself changing again, hacking away at space for myself,
breaking the green thoughts, trampling down the soft grass of my
    feelings,
diving into the silver waterfall of my soul and letting the momentum
of the word hurl me downstream, until I am found unconscious
    on a deserted
beach where sand and brittle prairie weeds stretch out. Then,
    here, I can
start again, to awaken in myself the meaning of a man's
smile, the utter contentment of death, blazing over at midday,
    over things
that have conquered their limits and know how to live in the
    smallest degree,
bring the red cactus blossom out on a full-moon night, without
    analysis,
without wondering . . . but knowing its beauty like a black stone
    caught
and grafted into the root. The knowledge of solitude.

                    *   *   *

These days I'm so busy with children, with trying to pay bills,
    with keeping
ahead of the bill collector. On the go, between broken old cars,
    worming
my dog, buying hundred-pound feed sacks of Hi-Pro cattle feed,
    spackling
the ceiling edges of each room, unplugging the drain and other
    endless chores,
between them all, like the snow stripping leaves each day, I must change
myself, prepare myself for the cold winter of the soul, for the
    hour when
I am nothing again, and I want to learn to talk again with the
    stone in my yard.

My hand turns slow but it turns, destroying the golden
objects in my life.
The earthquake of my dark tongue unfolds a cry of a human pain
through the green composed valley of the brain. And for an instant
all I enjoyed and loved I see false and broken, temporal debris
sucked back into earth. I am the food for the tornado that leaps
into cities and tumbles buildings down. I am the food that starves
    myself
until I eat the air of a very sunny morning.

Thirteen

I'm sitting here alone. It's the middle of the night, with memories
    of you and thoughts of you
interjecting themselves into my mind, my heart clenching a hope
    for your love
        as if hope were a gray strand of rope, shredded, nothing to
            hold the weighty sadness
        of being separated from you,
            wondering about you out in the desert, under the starry sky,

                    snuggled in your sleeping
bag—
        I want to kiss your feet, rub your legs, caress your thighs
                and inner legs with the greatest
attention
                and intent of conveying my sweetness all over you.

        I felt like reading Neruda's *Viente Poemas de Amor*
        before writing you,
        I felt like maybe I could say what I feel knotted in my heart
        if I read Hemingway,
                        but there's nothing
                        to explain a year with you
                        to describe the joy I felt
                        to know I was alive when I was with you.
        I don't have words to tell you what I'm feeling tonight
        I don't want sky space or stars or promises or food or music
                        I want nothing
        but this silence that permeates my face, my hands, my soul
        and lulls it into a peace
                        that offers me a reprieve from the passionate
                        and torturous sense of missing you.
        But you are in the desert.
        You left, promising me we would be together,
        that you would love me, that you would come back or I
                could come get you.
        You left.
        I don't recognize your voice, it's so filled with rage
        the rage of your rosebush exploding with stem thorns
                and bright red tight-unfurled roses.

You're right.
It is your life, your life, strumming with rhythms
of heaven-sent child wings,
your life, blue ice flakes
        that shimmer sun songs.

                        *   *   *

I wish tonight I could write what I want to say.
I don't want my life filled with people.
I don't want excitement and adventure for its own sake.
    I want quiet meditation
    in the mornings,
    I want to be alone
    with you.
When I first saw you in L.A., you pulled me into you,
a shy road dog in the bushes you lured out with your sweet
        words.
When we talked about being together,
I never wanted to tie you down, never desired to own or possess
        you
in a way that would hinder your beautiful flight,
    I wanted only to share my loneliness
    share my solitary ideas
    and memories
    with you,
        to laugh with you
as full and thick and unabashedly
as prairie grass in wind, leaning low with laughter,
scattering laughter like seeds to four directions,
laugh like cowboys slapping dust off jeans with cowboy hats,
laugh like being broncoed off a bull
and landing on the ground,
    then caressing as a child combs the mane of her horse at
        dawn,
    caressing you in every way
the wounds, the hurts, the doubts the pains the tears
caressing you
    as night fires lick flames to the edge of darkness,
    caressing the darkness.
I just wanted you
to ride with me through Chama and have a bowl of chili,
I needed no magic or prayer,
    I had you,
you were the mountains where my loneliness vanished,

you were my beautiful woman.
    I wanted to buy a house for us so you could rise at dawn
        and we could walk to the corner coffee shop,
      to travel with you,
      to watch you dance, to watch you heal,
      I would stand in awe of your power,
      your heart,
and all I ever wanted was someone to trust,
to be true to, to be hers,
    all I ever wanted
    was to care for you tenderly,
for you to know my heart, my fears, my childhood terrors,
as I clung to you and loved you
    the way you hunger to be loved.

I have my garden now to tell my secrets to,
I have my leaving this city and leasing my house
and going away to tell my sorrows to,
the night in faraway houses where I'll sit and compose poems,
I'll return to my real life of writing poems, of being alone, of being
attentive to the breathing of nature,
    keeping in mind how much I love you and desire you.

This is not a letter intended to convince you to return to me,
you go on your way, woman,
you have your family, you have your friends, you have your work,
but as I prepare to leave, telling no one a thing,
not a single human being knows my plans, I feel my heart like a
    brown sparrow
that's never flown before but is prepared to take flight
into the night
    and be alone in its flight, spiraling, gliding, in its own aerial
      dance
    of the Chicano blues
    for the woman it loves,
again,
this is not a letter to convince you of anything—

I remember in the mountains against the tree where I took you,
I remember the cold streams we bathed in,
the hot pools when you held me up and for the first time in my life
I felt loved and felt I could trust a human being on earth,
how the red-blood harvest moon completely overshadowed the
      alfalfa fields
on that country road through the Sangre de Cristos,
how I slept in your arms that night,
how we slept together in Cimarron, in that lovely old hotel
with animal heads anchored to the walls,

      but you have your life, your family,
      your friends to talk over your problems with,
      your friends to dance and party and make love to and share
            stories with,

and I am, at last, I think, understanding
how to be alone and appreciate the beauty of the view—
it's not flying to London to stay with a friend and write a play,
it's not traveling to Ecuador to tour the Galapagos,
      but to be loved and love
      and be near and care and cherish and plan your life
      with the one you love;
nor is it getting angry at me because you owe ten grand
on your damn credit card,
      those things are easily remedied.
      My love, you are an artist, surrounded by painters and
            writers and poets,
      and yet you don't know
you are truly the poet, my love,
and while all your wild women friends prowl bars to fuck strangers,
they don't know you are the artist,
they don't know that your emotions are like nights with volcanoes
exploding, like flowers in the desert blooming,
they don't know that you are more
      than all the tequila bottles and men you fuck,

you are more than all the employers who hire you,
you are more than your father sees, more than your mother
realizes,
more than your sister and brother will ever think you are,
because you were blessed, you are sacred, woman, you are a river
that washes out a town, a wind that blows the water tower down,
you have the old woman's wisdom, the young woman's passion,
the animal's lust for sniffing the dawn for food,
you dream such landscape and passion and love that no song will
ever capture your dreams,
and now
all I desire is sharing a sunrise with you,
holding your hand, listening to your thoughts,
wrapped in my arms,
I listen to your heart, to your breathing, I sniff your smell,
I absorb your touch,
I make a house for you, we travel, we love, we care for each
other
because life is so, so short, my baby,
wake the heart up
and in silence cross that magical line where we become one
rushing river downhill through canyons,
giving all, surrendering all, singing all,
away from the partyers,
from the drug users, the ambitious, the ones who
want to be writers and poets and dancers and
painters,
because you are,
and we breathe our beings—
you don't understand.
The cabin meant nothing.
Swimming in the pool in Washington meant nothing.
Driving roads all over New Mexico meant nothing.
The cabin in Taos. Nothing.
My house that made you feel like a woman, nothing.
The garden, nothing.

Your insincere gifts, nothing.
The altar I made for you to pray for your soul, because it is
    so precious, nothing.
The seashells, nothing but betrayal.
The hundreds of cafés and restaurants, nothing.
The crazy trips on California highways, nothing.
Peeing in the car, nothing.
Masturbating in the car on a country road, nothing.
The wonderful nights we made love, nothing.
The love and love and love and love and love
            NOTHING NOTHING NOTHING.

Book IV

Healing Earthquakes

One

Let's talk about our *hefitas,*
our great *madrecitas*
        who visit us in jail
bearing plastic bowls of home-cooked food,
    tortillas wrapped in towels,
        tamales y antojitos,
and at night pray for us on knees,
who gave us their breast milk,
    forgave us every crime
        even our *fassetas*
           carrying all love in their hearts for us.
    Employed for us,
        desde niños hasta hombres,
        hasta la muerte,
so respectful of the Mother Institution
we never made it human
or made our mothers human.
    Full of bitterness and weak from drudgery
    we kill each other when someone curses us,
    ¡Ah, chinga su madre!
    Guns ignite in every direction at those words
¿y 'pa qué?
You have ridden your mothers like proud pelicans on the backs
    of buffaloes,
    preening your feathers in the mirror,
    as she protects you from becoming chopping-block innards
        in the streets.

                *　*　*

I too have ridden my *madrecita* into
day and night,
a feathered eagle on her back as she fixed my meals,
        clothed me and washed me.
From the day I had my penis in her as an embryo
we have been in love with each other.
We are close to each other—
        if I were to kill someone
she would spend every penny for masses to ensure my soul
would not be condemned to hell.
And yet by the same token we hail our mothers
        as impeccable Virgin Marys
        and Guadalupanas,
        we seethe damnation on La Malinche
accusing every woman who doesn't want to fuck us
a *vendida* . . .
No entiendo Federico
in every woman are there two?
        Or on the back of our love is there hate?
        Dígame . . .
                do you think mothers were once women
                        needing love and affection in the bedroom
                                that would make them gasp with pleasure?

Or are they pleasureless beings?
Creatures who do not breathe air,
        who are not aware of our penises?
        Who are not aware that as children
                we found them foul and utilitarian
                        solely existing for our purposes
how we wished they could be more feminine
        and we grew watching them turn ugly before us
                their tits sagging to airless balloons
                        varicose veins worming their calves and thighs
                                their bras and panties in the bathroom
repulsed us

for we were children who denied these vestiges of their
        humanity
    for us they neither shit nor pissed nor slept
they were our *madrecitas*
        sexless virgins straining at the yokes of saintliness
        and they were to a degree
but oftentimes I smelled
        between my mother's legs
            she-bitch heat simmering
                    on a hot summer night
        there were times I saw my mother
        bare stepping out of the shower
with firm long legs
        and teeth marks on her breasts from a date the previous
            night
        love bruises along her inner thighs
where someone firmly gripped her and opened her full of love.
        When my mother put on makeup
eyeliner
        plucked brows
            and lotioned herself up,
she'd go out on a date, come back in drowsy dawn hours,
        sit next to me in bed and caress
my stomach with her man-smelling fingers, I could smell man-sex
        over her
        I recoiled from her
she became *La Malinche puta* who never cared for me
        and when she took off her black net stockings,
            sitting at the foot of her bed, I saw her unstrap her bra
                and she smiled and told me how I once suckled
                    her breasts.
        I wanted to suckle them again and crawl up inside her
        again
            and always be innocent.

But my innocence left me
        in the boys' shower room

when I started measuring my penis against other boys'
the one with the longest penis
          was the most macho man in the world
and those thoroughbred studs proudly walked with no towel
          around their hips
          back to their clothes
                    letting their cocks slap and slap against thighs
                              proudly hung firehoses
ready to devirginate any chastity vow
          and we boys were afraid to be caught looking at another
                    boy's penis
because wrong ideas might be had
          about how maybe we'd like it up our ass
and that be the case
          we wouldn't be men
so we kept our eyes purposefully away from the wrinkled collared
          cobra cock
          swaying from a bamboo basket of sparse puberty-age black
                    crotch hair
just ready to strike
          at the first bareheel walking past
          and as boys we had our rules
broke and made as warranted by circumstance and lust
          and yet to my mother all she could ever talk about was how dirty
men were and boys
          by virtue of having cocks.

Having a cock made you an animal
          I half believed her
          because at night most of the boys I knew
          jacked off under blankets
or went further at other boys' houses and while five and six boys
          to a bed slept
          there'd always be a hand snaking up someone's shorts
          feeling for a hard-on
and if not there, then attempting to make one . . .
          And I remember I never wanted to potty-train

not when I had my mother bending down by my hard-on
holding my penis and showing me gently how to pee
    and zip my pants
    and if I could have, I never would have learned to potty-train
the feeling of my mother's gentle hands on my penis
    made me feel wanted and desired
    made going to the bathroom
a sensuous adventure and somewhere inside me
    something shivered with pleasure and wanted to go further
    wanted me to be bigger and understand all the dark shadows
    crossing my blood
dark-suited scuba divers under the hull of a boat at night
    in the harbor lights.
    Yes I wanted to make love to my *madrecita*
    she was Guadalupe and Malinche
filth and purity in one woman
      holding my penis teaching me to pee
and how I loved peeing in my pants and having her call me from
    the swings
           to go through this love ritual.

But even that changed,
    her beauty paled, a horse beaten once too many times with a
        whip
    she seemed old and unenchanting
soup kitchen serving maid
    with mean jowls at the corners of her lips
    scolding me constantly as I grew older
and perhaps, as I once thought, she led me to believe she desired
    me on several
    occasions.
I caught her spying on me dressing, sometimes in front of the mirror
I would rub my stomach muscles, ease my stiff cock
down in my pants off to one side a scabbard on a saddle
ready to fit a woman's hand down inside
once at the movies
    she felt the same lust in her I guess

I felt once watching her step out of bed
those brown nipples
chocolate-kiss teardrops I wanted to melt on my tongue
and being macho
I never expressed this to anyone
I lived in silence as if there was no part like this in me.

I was always scared of being naked, of others seeing my naked skin
having to dress as a kid with all my skin covered
from wrists to ankles covered
naked skin was bad, penis was a devil stick
males had to have our penises cut off to be pure
hide them into little shriveled pigs' tails in our crotches
because to expose the penis or see the penis or fondle the penis
would warrant everlasting hells of fire
unforgiving wrath of God and I was scared,
I was carrying around a bad deformation,
a terrible curse
called a penis.
It didn't belong to me
this penis came flying out of space one night while I slept
and I couldn't pull it off
it just stuck to me
a root
grown up out of the ground
and when I woke up this penis root
was growing from me instead of earth.
And the women were mad at that because they looked at me
strange
I could tell coming down for breakfast with a hard-on in
my shorts
my *madrecita* looked at me crossly . . .
The penis was an evil tool of the devil
that it should be clubbed a nasty python
thrown off one of those pilgrim ships
have all those founding criminals that came from England
in the ships

fill cask after cask with brimming penises before they hit land
    writhing buckets of worms
    toss them into the sea
    to scuttle ocean bottoms and eat coral reefs and be eaten
by sharks for lunch
    have no boy or man with a penis in this puritan
Episcopalian country
    they thought would make us worthy of heaven and I
        thought so too
but you know that was impossible.

And more than that, I knew I was condemned from the gate
    because when the lights went off
    and people snored
    I went to masturbating
a hundred-yard-dasher breaking record after record
    for crossing the ribbon
    of my semen
across the whole room in fine squirts of pelvic spasmodic jolts of
    pleasure
    I was a devil
    damned to be shackled
and whipped by God's dark wolves in hell
and for this manly pleasure, naively and feeling mountains of guilt
    I meekly admitted I loved masturbation
    and smartly admitted
grown-ups were wrong about most things
    they were probably wrong about masturbation too.
My penis grew long and swollen-veined like other men's
    my fear of it being a stunted acorn
    left me.
I began to look at it, awed
    at how beautiful it was, how smooth and swan-sleek its profile
    how good it felt in my hand
    how wonderful to fondle it
    how unspeakably dazzling coming was at such a young age
        in the toilet stall . . .

But everybody I knew
        said the body was bad
        and I felt mine was a towel every ogre and troll
                and devil had wiped their evil hands on—
Mother told me my body was prone to filthy deeds and foul ways
        that my dick would lead me to hell if I followed its pointing
(it pointed upward, not down)
        all her scolding ever did was make my head go way down
in the hallways and classrooms at school, while everybody else's
        heads were held high
        mine was bobbing at my knees in shame.

        I believed them all
                and believed in a world
                        where babies came from under beds,
drawn to the dust-mop lint dust
        just born one night or morning
                like a zit on my chin.
        I believed no man ever
                        put his dick into a woman
        I never knew what they called the vagina
                to me women were smooth between the legs
                        like plastic dolls on Woolworth's racks
I believed all people just appeared one moment as babies and grew
        and somehow I had to find a way to cut off my penis
        because it kept growing bigger than an ear of corn
golden-tasseled with cum when I saw a woman strutting in a tight
        red dress
        cum all over myself when I saw
the panties of a girl walking up the stairwell in front of me
        my head level with her buttocks
        me clicking my teeth like her black high heels chattering
on the steps . . .
        I was really misinformed somewhere about this whole sex stuff.

Two

One day the priest me asked to change the garments
on the saints in church.
    I refused.
    He slapped me, pushed me toward the side altars roughly and
        demanded I change their clothes. I said no.
He reached up and took St. Francis and Our Virgin Mary
    shoved them in my arms then walked away.
    When I undressed her I lay down with her in the pew
and held her in my arms and rested.
    I kissed her cheeks and combed her hair and spoke with her
she held me back and embraced me.
    Days after that, every time I looked at the Virgin
    the question of whether she had a place
between her you-know-what
    kept imaging in my mind
    and I prayed hard to wipe away the picture of her
        with nothing on
    I really tried not to commit a mortal sin
    but every time I prayed to her
she appeared naked to me, nine years old, loving me
    and every time I prayed to Christ
the same thing, except his male thing
would be always in the way and I tried to obfuscate it, I tried to
    ignore it
    I tried passionately to pray harder
        but there it was hanging
            or upraised stiffened and his you-know-what
                seemed to get in the way of my praying
      so I stopped praying

just couldn't think of his having a you-know-what like me.
I wondered why nobody else was seeing what I was
    trying not to see
    why these common human traits never occurred to anyone
        but me
    and I thought myself the most vile profane hideous monster
        ever allowed to breathe on earth.
    I hated myself, hated my skin
    hated my eyes and penis and hated my lust, hated
    everything sensuous and soft and physically loving
    and hating it all, I knew I was lying to myself because I
        loved my body
loved the idea of giving myself pleasure
    in a world of people
        who could only detest and berate anything human.
I found myself masturbating every night
    and going to mass every morning
caught in a vicious vortex, a snarling shark's mouth
    of guilt and pleasure
        even looking at my palm in the light some days
            wondering when it was going to fall off
    or when I would become an amputee or ape
             dragging my knuckles on the sidewalks
    and sooner or later I would be shot
    because I was just too damn evil for loving my body
when everybody else hated theirs
    and it seemed nobody else knew sex existed except me as a boy
    every time wind blew
up a woman's dress my eyes were two black birds
    on the two roseate peach cheeks beneath her panties
    when a woman crossed her leg just so
meekly and covertly I averted my eyes to see up her crack
    into that forbidden dark moist crevice
where I believed all love and pleasure and ecstasy was kept
    and their long glance sent me into a hard-on hysteria
    and there was temptation everywhere.

*   *   *

I was a young leper boy
        thinking my skin a diseased oozing sore
        thinking I was the worst
                        of all possible demons
        and my boy heart filled with fear
at any time God would strike me down and blast me into dust
        for thinking and feeling
                        a young boy's normal sensations . . .
I was worse than spit-bucket bile my uncle suffering from
        pneumonia
        retched out.
        I tried to repent
by praying, by thinking I was scum, keeping my eyes lowered,
        forcing the worst
                        jobs on myself
saying all the time I deserved punishment, I deserved to die and
        be stripped of
                        of my skin slowly with whips
                        made of cactus needles.
        I deserved to be left in the mountains
                to freeze to death
                and be eaten by vultures
and even that would be too good
        and I learned to hate myself
                        hate all things
                        that came from the dirty body
        be ashamed of my penis, try to hide it
        and emotionally neuter myself
                        become a virtuous eunuch
        dipping my filthy hand that held my penis
                into the holy-water fountain in church
                closing my eyes with remorse that I was ever born.

Three

I held women in such high esteem
    untouchable
    and wondered why they went at night flying across cities
    to faraway places
                to do mysterious things
    why they were not as brute and carnivorous as I
        why they kept all their beauty to themselves
    alone, pristine gardens
somehow connected to me.
      They belonged to another world of holiness and virtue and
        sublimity

                              my eyes devoured—
    we were too different
    they were light in the haunting tunnels of my heart
    they were jewels
in dark treacherous hands, and while they sailed the rest of the world
    I squirmed and snarled and gnawed
    they were magical, could do things to me by entering my view
        make me have an erection without recognizing me
          without acknowledging my existence
             and my heart groveled for attention
    every inch of their flesh gave a bottomless brightness
    I wanted to adore.
I wondered when and where and what made them draw off their masks
    take off their clothes
            and make love.
I wanted to be everything that triggered their lust
    but I was dumb and ignorant and mute
        cursed to hate my body

to never allow its expression
half a man
and as I grew
I had to get drunk and high to sit at a table and
talk with a woman
had to desensitize myself
to my own self-hate and fear
with whiskey and grass just to talk with a
woman
because everything between us
was illegal and immoral
destined to be cursed by the world
and so I ignored woman,
my hands horrid appendages of evil
claws or hooves of the devil
meanly scratching at the hard earth.
Woman and I
always kept apart
I remember no adult could sit a girl on his lap
without everybody suspecting his motives
no girl could be alone with a man
we were always kept apart
girls with girls and guys with guys
and even if you wanted to be with a girl
custom forced you to be with guys otherwise you weren't
one of the guys
I never guessed women could howl and scratch and pant
and lunge
in the fucking better than any man
we learned to express our lust
on Saturday night
by beating the shit out of one another, by drinking so much
beer and wine
we passed out
by telling untrue stories about women
to abate our horniness
we joshed at each other about tiny dicks and cocksuckers

about how some men were manless wimps
              tight-assed frigid toe-sucking assholes
all this came out in half-bleary grins
                    and we all slept horny on couches
in rooms littered with beer cans and record jackets of
         Hendrix and Joplin
lying all over
         cigarette and marijuana stubs in ashtrays
         and the morning another dreary womanless loveless
awakening
              and hating the smell of men, the sour stench of beer breath
and no softness
                    our covert lust
                         became distorted
         cruising the Country Club area for girls
         putas
         with Grand Canyon acne and sucked-in buns and cavernous
              addicts' cheeks
all hallowed-eyed
         chunks of lipstick at lip corners
         eyeliner so thick one could draw hopscotch outlines on
              their foreheads
hair so stiff
         it seemed baled in a baling-wire machine
                   blue-haired bitches and platinum blondes
                        willing to fuck for a bottle of Tokay
         set 'em on the hood of the car in the alley
                   lift their dresses and fuck
done in minutes
         out again cruising thinking that somehow what we did
                   bordered on love
         it was what we were taught and allowed to know
         about love caged in bodies
         we knew nothing, nothing and women taught us
              to hate who we were
         and now we are sharing the hate with them again

two human beings hating each other's bodies out of fear
and we call it love.
And those bitches on car hoods and at the proms and movie dates
eventually became our
park girlfriends
we took the vaginal juice and lipstick
as true love
and we would have killed for those lips on our lips only
and those thighs
fat and cottony and slimy ones, candy sticky with semen
only ours.

Four

This is the education I got
from you women and men
to hate every part of the body
idolize every woman
as inhuman
mannequin
for gawking men
for hooting construction workers to jeer and catcall . . .
but when a woman looked back at us with all that moon-growling
jaguar power
something in me quivered weakly and asked for mercy
because women had a dark fermenting power
able to make me flee to a dark corner and hope they never found
me . . .
when I caught love edge in their eyes
peering down at me
I had to find a place to hide.

We had Planned Parenthood
in the alley, in the boxing gym, in the backseat,

everyone around me fucking everybody else
    I had missed love
        with all my abstinence
            my holiness trying to be pure and humble and
                modest
while everyone around was fucking, I was the only one on the street
me and a few other guys
    but everyone else
    in living rooms
    in trees
    under bridges
    under cars, behind walls
    in touchdown zones
    whole world fucking
    except me
    with my image problems
    and a hard-on.

First time I had sex
    I was a swollen hundred-year rain brimming a river channel
    overspilling the pubic shores of this girl's purring pussy
    twisting and grunting and grinding
    riveting pain piercing my groin and penis
    blood all over the sheets
    thinking the blood hers until I asked, no
    I checked myself and found I'd ripped my foreskin . . .
even in pain
    all I could ever think about was fucking
    it was all over, with me thinking it was illegal
it was the most legal and proper thing to do
sex was it.
    Every day opened like a huge ripe mango
    sliced in half
    having the pattern of a pussy
single hours had legs of a woman stripping off nylons that clung
    to the
    second hand on the school clock

the whole world had reduced itself to pussy and cock
     connecting in sweaty ooze sap and slicing flesh-sty
     we stripped our clothes off, potato skins peeled off
we fried hot sizzling scalding raw burning each other in grunts
     with youthful lust . . .

Past teaching told me inside
     woman-pussy was fish wrapped in newspaper and left too
          long
on the bin in warm weather between their thighs
     not to be touched or seen
     just insert the penis without looking
     or touching and cum
and this teaching took me the first time I bent my head between
     a girl's legs
     taught too I suppose not to wash there
because I puked and gagged back all the teaching
     and tried to persuade myself it wasn't true
     how bad flesh was
     how terribly bad flesh was
     how awful
     and sinful it all was . . .
     trying to hold my breath back from the smell
     trying to learn how to lick
     until the girl sat up and we taught each other
throwing shame and humiliation under the bed
     we made our minor adjustments
     and when songs came on, I cried
     and when I was alone in my room
     I cried
     and felt myself all alone in this world
     no woman could ever love or like me
I knew and understood nothing, there was something terribly
     wrong with me
     and I cried in the dark for hours and hours
listening to the whole world outside my window
a world of men and women with each other

and me so lonely I tried to make-believe I was courageous enough
        to think suicide
        but couldn't
because I had never had anyone love me
        love the person I was
        and I had never felt love from anyone
        never felt someone care for me
and before I died
        I wanted to try and find out if there was something like that
            on earth
        and all around me men were finding love
        in bullets they died from
        in fights they bled in
        in bones they broke
        in hate they spewed
        in racism they snarled
        in fast cars crushed around streetlamp poles
        in cases of beer and LSD
        in music
        there was love everywhere
except between men and women.
        I saw women love guys
        who could shoot a ball through a hoop
        others loved cowboys who could spit tobacco
        others loved the brain
        others who loved pit-bull mugs and chains in pockets
        others loved men for their shirts and shoes and teeth and hair
        I was looking for love that came from the heart
        and there was none.

        Most of the hearts I felt
        were mushrooms grown in the dark
        you bit into and were poisoned
girls and guys screaming at each other
        fucking out of spite
        fucking dumb and blind drunk
        fucking because there was nothing better to do

bored of their meaningless lives
    so they fucked
    and jocks fucked because it was what football heroes did
after a game
walked around sore-balled, hemorrhoidal-bow-legged and
    arm-bulky gruesome
    trolls
    girls seemed to love
smelling of jockstraps and dirty sneakers
    girls reveled in
    looking for love
wondering what was wrong with me, a tender soft-spoken fearful
    gentle boy
    I was
    ready for the picking
    filled with luscious sweet juice and warm browned intimacy
I was alone out here
    repressing love urges saying I had to be good
    had to be quiet
    stalk a woman like a tiger
    take her down jungle-force
these things I couldn't do, I felt like talking about my blues
    felt like befriending a woman
    felt like she was my equal
and so I was against male thinking and male feeling ways
    I tried to blend in
    to the dirt
    and be no one
for a while
    be a cardboard
            box.

I didn't know where to put myself—
    where do you put a useless human being
    can't hang it in the closet
    or throw it outside

what do you with a useless human being who is a boy
    looking for love
away from the crowds like a hermit
        maybe do that Roman thing and give him a sword and
            shield
        and put him in the ring with lions
or slam him with the Sir Arthur knight on the search for the grail
next best thing for me was jail
        county jail
        was as far as I could get out of a society where I didn't
            belong.
I could talk to growling men
        who'd fought for and lost their dreams
        better than I could talk to women
but I had to have bars before me to keep me from roaming and
            asking questions
        out too far and getting lost in my loneliness again
        seeing everyone with a woman but me
I preferred the dark cage
        to open parks with everyone hugging and lying down with
            their girls
        I preferred the dying to the living
        the crying to the laughing
and it all started way back when they said to me my body was no
            good
        just a hateful piece of trash to get rid of
        the sooner the better.

Five

There was a time I despised
everything Chicano, lowering my eyes meekly afraid of admitting
        my father was Mejicano and my mother Indian
I was small-boned and thin with large blueberry eyes and raven hair

I was the dark spot of ink on the white world
    blond-haired Viking-boned Wheaty-chortling kids
    drank Borden milk and blue cornmeal *atole*
I had a cactus-fiber *mecate* belt
they had new leather and new shoestrings
    I walked on my heels and they walked on toes
they wore JCPenney T-shirts
    and I, khaki work shirts with the cuffs rolled
grease and bike oil under my fingernails and bitten cuticles
    I was cholo'd to the *juesos* prim
my world wrapped in the meat cutter's milky wax paper
    my *abuelita* unwrapped the soup bones from to make *caldo*
I wanted to scrape off any sign of my Chicanismo
    like my teeth scraped off bits of meat from each bone
at my school desk I saw the Gavos had the whitest socks
at the bus stop they drove by with mamas in nice heated cars
    CBS commercial to the bone carnal
my *shante* was black wood rotten Osha root birds and horses
    chewed and pecked on
    through the board cracks I could see stars at night
my *shante* was chewed root
    and I denied who I was, afraid to raise my head
because the shit-kickers with Big Time Wrestling belt buckles
    tattooed on my skin
    embossed bronc and arm-swinging cowboy rider
and everybody wanted to be what they were not
    my Chicano language changing to a nasal whine, some version
of a West Texas ballroom blonde talking
    I was ashamed, *vato*, because all the older role models
too were ashamed, I could sense it, and instead of looking
    outward anymore
    sabes que carnal, sabes que,
    deep in me, behind all the shame and contradictions
I heard faint scratchings of First Mother, Mother of Us All,
    and I saw her in my dreams
    black thing, with one eye, hairy arms and body,
    squatting, tits bare, mean savage *madrecita*

Meztiza
       a *niño* on the dirt before her fire
       she fingered mud-leaf gruel in my mouth
       a hairy twisted-faced deformed-hand glittering dark-jeweled eyes
brown scratched scabbed-flesh Mother of Us All
            gooing me, mangy furred toenails encrusted with moss scum
            diseases oozing from thigh
            legs buffalo-rough
she grunts me on knees, knocks my head with her hands urging
       me to walk
or cry, she cradles me in her thorny arms and I drink her milk
       while I suckle
       I hear in her throat grumbling low rumbles of threats
       to unseen intruders in bushes
and when I finish she snugs me under her arm
       and we go walking, her thighs crooked wide and bowed
she steps full of stink and insect bites, she steps me on up the
       tree
just a dream, you see, in which she was ready to give her life for me
a fearful, always being scolded, battered by hostile grown-ups,
       nonexistent boy,
       betraying my own blood hip to exchange my culture for
       pirate Vikings and white-thighed women
       straining back their bow-and-arrow gutstring
to slay a bronze man
       with my Chicano face
       Olmec-Toltec *cara como tengo*
it's a wonder I didn't scar deeper and irrevocably, strip the
       intestines from me
       and leave me a bare canyon wall.

       I was scared to be me in America
       beneath my white talking
       white wanting
       white feeling
they told me
       got to carry a Bible, boy,

sho 'nough to be brown is to be damned, boy
and way deep in me
the Great Mayan Mother angrily scratched up dirt and threw it
    up in mourning
she was telling me not to die, telling me I have truth inside
    myself not others
telling me I got rituals
    and when I listened, Lord,
my telling became rude, cave-calling howls of sweet child chants!
    I threw sticks at new cars
      ate leaf buds off elm trees on Sunset Road
and by virtue of listening to the lion-leafed First Mother in me
    I relearned to click my taps on shiny school halls
      no Hush Puppy classroom yap boy here
I was tacked bull's-eye on every social worker's corkboard as DV
    Delinquent Villain
I changed to Defiant *Vato*
with a grunting First Mother who stripped meat from elk bones
    with her fingers
    and fed me bloody *oso tripas*, o yeah
and this poetry emanates afterkill heat of opened jaguar mouth
when in a dream
    First Mother was chased, attacked, criticized
First Mother and I, grungy, growling festering bitch First Mother
    and I
    up-swamp *llorona* guttering volcanoes
    of uttering love from her for me drooling deeply cut lips
how different I was,
    Madrecita
    I learned to use fire by burning down courthouses
    to protect myself
in the same way you picked up fire against predators
    amidst all the chest-beating wally-lolling tongue-sucking
        hatred
toward me
    I learned to camouflage myself white
    impishly scurrying along baseboards

becoming a golden-bowled fish for them to look at
        but I survived solely by the dream, with the Great Mother
            of Us All
brown haggard bitch picking fleas from my hairy belly
        my First Mother and Mother of All
my relationship to her
made others think me a failure and insignificant
        her licking my wounds and grave somber eyes
        made the white world
a failure
        I disregarded
until you handcuffed me
        zoo cargo and boxed me up in neat paragraphs
and slapped a sticky tag on me I could never get off.

        More I got to know of First Mother's tenderness
        the way she scratched up a hole in the dirt to shit, the way
            she covered
it, the way she rubbed and caressed a tree, the way she played
        with leaves on her tongue,
the way she scratched herself and let me run wild, let me jump on
        her back
        more angry I became at women and men
        in defense of my Great Bitch Mother who stood on hind legs
and howled in defense of me
        a self-hating Chicano
        getting beat up and going hungry
        afraid to go to sleep, terror was so bad
while droves of Chicanos abandoned barrios under the Johnson
        grant era
        leaving their nos behind and taking their yesses
to college and business schools
        with a chance to speak out and they don't
        black shoreline hearts
        molting Chicanismo off
        strutting high on Rockefeller Grants and Fulbrights

bow-wowing good-bye
    to the barrio homegrown *vatos y rucas*
    dentures gleaming
tenured toothlessness
    smiling deny deny
on limping pride and handkerchiefing a feigned cough
    in look-away crowds
    turning back from the bus stop
    from the barrio
    from our *cultura*
but no one can exist
not long
    denying truth
and it must have taken only a little time
        until that rage from deferred to as a dummy bean
    took fuse
must have been only a little time for that rage to ignite
    cold-shocking you with the sham
you must have been mad
running from so much to something so unreal
    and me annoying you
    with my First Mother grunts
    exiling yourself from who you are
    from the spirit of Teotihuacan and Tonantzin
you erupted
sun shed its bark and the year of the dragon came upon us
    in fiery concentric surf-fire smoldering waves
    and I sympathize with you
but still, known for my meek and humble character
    I take your insults and violent temper and academic sniper shots
    you went through much and I forgive you
forgive you your dream of being rich
while I fix up my '64 Chevy low-rider
bumper hardly clearing a speck of sand
so low
    not one of them educated cars
    with voices and directions and computers

you drive back on Sunday and visit the barrio a hero of success
    with a check that makes you feel good
    and a fine Norwegian woman's leg wrapping you from waist
        to shoulder
    you snap-buckle loose man
who divorced a Chicana
    to fulfill the mirage of Mr. Successful
a blue-eyed Wonder Bread girl in each arm could make all the
    shame go away
uh-huh
    where you came from and who you are could vanish
    and you could call yourself a pure-bred white stallion
    blah blah blah
and at conferences from Chile to Anchorage you could say you're
    Spanish
    not a wisp of Indian blood
    you running on empty appearances
    bouldering bliss brawn willfulness
of a new era, decade of the 2000s, saying yes master at all the
    right times
    clomping those heavy expensive hooves into the twenty-first
        century
    rebelling from First Mother Ways and Dreams
    educating me not to back-talk
    issuing government grants or tenured favors
from your papal dais
    but no one is going to do me
    as I want to do me
this is what you did to your life, brother and sister
    this is what you did
hear my voice no longer wanting to be
    Mr. Successful.

    See my pain, because I'm facing it
    it hurts to be Chicano
I lie down on the pyramid altar and you peel back my skin and
    plunge your hand

into my heart
    finding the face of Our First Great Mother
all dark and scrawny and mean-looking, herb-gathering woman
        of mine
        and no matter how you armor yourself with New-Glow
            Whammie Ju-Jus
and shit work
        escaping First Mother
you walk outside on a January night and see the cold brilliant night
        horses sleeping on their feet, you note
        in the air
vapors of moon mist and white auras
        of the Great Dark Mother breathing her breath into your lungs.

She lives in my male impulse, in the brown melancholy of skeletal
        trees
        and bids me to bear myself up on two feet, on heart, on soul
        declaring myself to the world
all of us spring from her, in all our human filth and grotesque
        warring instinct
in all our inimitable beauty, we are human beings of One
        Mother . . .

    And now I think of men
    breaking their bonds
who have a right to become hysterical
        who claim a calmness now
        ritualizing their lives
        with male fertility.
I remember I made love to Lisana
        soon as I came into her I felt a deep loss,
        soon as I gave myself to her I lost my value, my seed
felt a wound cleaving me
        soon I lost my self-esteem
        giving myself to you
why?

I sent flowers and letters afterward, but always between us
    were the unwritten words
and we crushed leaves of ourselves in our hands
    smoke that never caught the kind of flame we wanted
    why?
I bow to the First Mother and have work to do—
    First Mother who grunts, points, sniffs,
    claws up earth in me
    howls prayers to the sun
teaches of God, how God lives in us all
    how our spirits are sparks in water
    doused to ashes
she rubs on her face
    attempting to show me love—
                the relationships
                between men and women—
Ahoa!

Six

I grew up around John Wayne, thinking he was
    a wolf trapper and a woman was a pelt
    he slung over his shoulder
    pussy carcass
or General Custer
    taking pussy
    like he was counting scalps
    or Daniel Boone
trapping beaver and snaring him some
    and back at his cabin he tells another frontiersman
    Caught me fourteen pussies today . . .
that mentality
thrives in truck drivers and policemen and judges and lawyers
    the lofty pillared founding men of this country

crave woman one moment and the next scorn her
as a throwaway thing—
and then woman spoke out—
You got to carry a knife
because you can't talk
you got to carry a gun
because you fear your own shadow
you got to be and act like you're tough
because you're a child
lost in a world
you don't know how to make choices
you don't know which way to go
you don't know enough to open your eyes, man

because you're afraid of woman
you're afraid of woman blood
afraid of woman saying you're shit
she won't dirty her finger on your dust
much less blow it off the windowsill.

And underneath it all, man
I'd paint you up with lipstick   ·
take my eyeliner and paint your lashes and beneath your guarded eyes
rouge your cheeks
smear some sweet-smelling lotion on your face
powder-puff your hairy belly
and make you all sweet-smelling cuddly soft
and take you down bawling on the ground
and you would love it all
you would love it all
pretty boy you are a pretty thing
you are
so afraid you got to hide from me
so afraid you got to prove you a man
you don't know what you missing being a man . . .
And then man spoke back—
. . . no woman is going to tell me what to do

who pays the rent
        who works in the rain
        who gets up and puts on the pants
        who's going to tell me
not a woman
        she's got to pay heed and mind me
        she got to do what I say
no thinking and feeling
        no backtalk
        no idea about another way
no woman is going to tell me what to do
why I slap the bitch down crawling in her puke and blood
why I kick that bitch down
        licking her tears off my boot tips
        why
I run this house
        this roof
        this floor
        this food
        this life
I give to her as a master gives life to a slave
        why no woman
is going to tell me what I can do and can't do
why water don't run uphill
        it runs down her pants
        she squats while I stand
        she opens while I come
        she's silent while I talk
        she is mine to do what I want to do with
        you hear?
And woman answered—
        Jealousy is going to kill you
        thinking about when I go visit a friend
a man friend
        you think
I can live only with spread legs on his couch

while I suck his cock
     jealousy is going to kill you
thinking about his hand on my brown nipples
twirling around the bud in his thumb
     lollying my nipple in his mouth
sucking in the whole melon
jealousy's going to kill you, boy
     thinking a woman can go visiting only to get laid
she goes seeing and walking and sleeping and eating only
     to fuck
is going to kill you
     thinking my between-legs place
is for all the world to fuck and chew and eat and spit and take and touch
     but you
thinking that
     is going to kill you, boy!

Then man replied—
     You know a bitch'll lie
     she'll keep that pussy straying
to make you beg
     but they'll betray
     and they'll connive
     and fuck your best friend
     smiling toothy teeth at you
serving you coffee
     in the morning
     and serving up pussy to your best friend
     at noon.
Yes sir
     they'll betray
     don't trust a bitch no more than a bullet your way
     she'll come behind you and rip out your wallet
     rip out your heart
     telling you she's lighting candles at a local church
     she'll be damning your cursed soul to hell
     with folded hands and on knees.

Seven

I spoke of the dragon rising from the earthquake.
Dragons do not care in my bones
    o Lord, do not care about shame
    the clean grunt from the bowels
        when they fuck
            geyser smoke sperms up
hisses and sizzles continents
collide and rack in fucking quakes.
    I have things to say to women—
    dragon words
    gut-crunch claw-dripping growl
because women have been stepping on me.

It's just why we can't get together
    can't get closer than humping crotch on crotch
    then throwing chairs and swearing and leaving me drinking
    staring up at them sweet stars and whispering
    Lord, why can't we get the blues squeezed out of our toes?
Yes,
    I grew up around locker-room talk
    how a man beat a woman down
    with a fist clenching as much love as ever
    grew up and grew down
    with locker-slamming ball players
    snapping wet towels on the ass 'n' back
    yooing and yeowing sweet male ass
    grew up
    'round oil driller's oily hands and face
    talking pipe pussing down in that hole

men's hands grinding it down, holding steady
    down in that black-salt fish-smelling slime-glimmering wet
        mother juice
'cause we just 'tave it
    he said
and swigged his apricot wine from a mason jar
and slept
    and I got problems 'n' no one to talk with
    homegrown boy
    nourished on mean-tempered people and ass-whacking bitches
    I took they shame on me
    they didn't have nowheres else to put they shame
    they put it in me
like rain wet my hair
they shame wet my soul
like mud-slogged shoes going to work
my slogged heart kept moving
    like doors never open to me
    like horses hoofing dirt to find baby shoots of sprout grass
their shame never allowed me my full green, never did that.
    I'm angry about that, them putting they shame on me.
And you know why we have to talk, me and women?
    Because I want to get physical
    and emotional
    no love intending bending my bones, just lust
    my toes ache with anger
    anger backed up in my throat like hair in grease in a pipe trap
and my dick talks
    I listen
    on the bus
    in the workplace
    on the bed
    on the spoon filled with beans and in my bread 'n' butter
    my dick talks
ain't no love
    just lust
and you say it wrong?

Let me tell you something about men, honey
        not one doesn't dream about fucking until the legs won't
            hold you up
too weak in the groin crotch
        not one of their dicks don't start sliming shorts at seeing
swaying heat-radiating electric bone-blinding meat-heating bitch
        howling
        down the street the way you do
        I know. I am a man.
        You'd like to paint me up to slim your fear of my male need
        paint my lips paint my cheeks paint my eyelashes
and cuddle me up puppy-warm and milk-whiskered
        brown-eyed
        in your lap
        uh-huh
women lubby-lipped wet panting panties make me believe
                you
                        you don't
but I know better.

        You hear this talk is what I learned growing up
        how I learned to see you women
        remember the first time I stepped on that dirt bridge
        walking proud to see you
        water and all hell abounding, waves curling and drowning
                up around me
        and me and my feet dry just walking up to you
        when all of a sudden the land bridge gets flooded
        I drown.
        O woman, you tried to drown me in your sneaky betrayal
        tried to swallow me up in your lips and blow me out,
                smoke rings
on the air
        afraid to touch my skin on your heart
        afraid of my disease which is nothing more than lust
and you

bucking like a rodeo mare, all lathery between the thighs
just wanting to lift that tail
and snort and kick and bite and rear and lash
I know, I am a man.
You got to understand us men, women, that there isn't
anything wrong with lust.
We like the immediate feeling
having our dicks squeezed dry
having thighs and breasts and lips and buttocks and legs
all pressed against us
we feel like Magi Indian Guru
silk-bound and pillow-traveling
on heaven's bodily bliss and jeweled vision, honey
just by you and your body.

But everywhere women are sharpening their teeth
saying what I learned is wrong.
Maybe so, maybe so.
O, you shamed me enough for reaching out innocent enough to
grab your ass
O, you humiliated me enough reaching out innocently to rub
your tits
O, you angered me as I reached out to caress your nipples
in fondness, in loving fondles and decent gentleness
you just snarled, you just turned white, you just told me
what a no-good muthafucka I was
why I didn't have a goddamn grain of a brain to know better
why I was worse than a cannibal
why you wouldn't talk to me for days
with you parading that pussy across me like a New Orleans
showboat
ignoring a drowning man at sea
and you don't want to give me a helping hand and I'm
drowning
I don't understand this conundrum, honey.

*   *   *

Not a man alive never choked his turkey
        gobbling
        to climb a fine mare when his hunger struck hot licking his nuts
finger flame
        itching him
        messing with his heart and mind and soul
        at the sight of a fine pair of tits and them humming
back ends
        buzzing men's bones to act like hives of bees on the first
            day of spring
no man alive, no ma'am.
        We just haven't talked.
        I know. You wish to sew my lips shut
        with a thread of your hair
        run that thread through my lips just lusting hiss for you
        well, I bet you would clip your fingernails to a needle
and thread my lips shut
        because man's talking now
better than shaming me
        because man's talking now
better than humiliating me
putting your righteous blame on me
        instead of where it belongs
        out there
        away from me and you
        out there
        away from me and you.

        We men have a problem, men and women
got a problem.
        You have been mad-dogging and crew-cutting
        cud-chewing men
to shreds
to spit out.
        I have nothing against you
        not a thing.
        Why all this hate and silence between us?

I'm sharing my education with you
who taught me to sip my coffee and stir in my sugar and milk
the way you sipped me and stirred in my semen
taught me to grind on you and you sit on me
        and to this day the loose bra strap feels better than any
                crepe-paper
bunting
        and the feel of my fingers drawing your panties down
        those cold firm thighs
was much better than slipping red bows off my Christmas presents.

        Men are crass
        ass-jawing two-penny punks
        wet-dicked mumbling cur-cringing blood-begging
                mold-green scum
who'll do anything for a cigarette
or a warm bed.
        But not this one
        I really loved when I loved you, woman
        loved out of you the cold blue icicles
        I really loved you
and you turned your face from me, tippy-toed to another man
        and I really loved you, woman
until I learned your track record for fucking others
        could have
fueled daily rockets to the moon and back for thirty years.
        I really loved you in my own rough dirty slime-pool way
like you never had love
        soul-cum given you drained me to nothing but
        a moment of you and me
        your vagina moving like a jungle flower
        my cum raining
        and you drinking it in
peeing all over the bed and me grunting like a saber-tooth getting
        his tooth pulled
        o, it was sweet Sunday simmering cock-food just roostering
        my heart with loud cockadoodledoo joy, woman!

Altar boy quiet with you
    my heart's whispering hem edge on the floor
you just dragged out of me
    dragged me out of my senses
    you made my heart a soft boiled potato
and I would have done just about anything
    and I have to explain a man's heart
    because I can't go anymore with you over there and me
over here.

    Coming-together time
    women and me.
    I'm no preacher on a milk crate
    preaching thirst to a dry-tongued drought-throated crowd
because I'll drop your drawers in the confessional, honey
give you absolution
    absolutely
    man-style
    hard and stiff man's staff, ho, Lord, ho!
Got to educate woman about who I am!
    Been too long
    you been blind about me.
I'm not talking about lollipop love
    I'm talking about how you women are burning men as witches
    noosing us up and if the horse don't run
    or we don't hang
    you tug on the legs, four or five of you
    make sure my neck pops.
I'm talking about those millions of men out there
silent, quiet, church-going-to-work faces
tax-ready men out there dying to tell it
    who have a lot of anger at you, woman.
Be glad you're not a man!
    Then you'd understand
    all the anger toward you

and all the love toward you, living love, ageless building
        love for you
    so much
you can protest this truth
        think we are animals for fucking
yeah
        fire up the kindling and burn me
        there's nothing like a woman's temper
hurricanes and typhoons squish mud out of islands, but a
        woman's temper
        can tamp a man in until he's nothing but a bug spot on the rug
        a pissing post for dogs
        a secondhand kicking junkyard tire to sell cheap
yeah
        and about right now
        you're feeling trigger happy, ball-crushing demolition-gear
            happy
        so many of you
run out of ink signing our execution papers
use your blood to sign the paper
        and nail men to the pyre to smoke his hide for good eating
        yes, I know.

Past your ordered eight-room house and tree-lined streets
        past the MAs and PhDs
and igloo-pure and innocent lives
        down onto the streets I take you
to smell that pussy again
and see that man cum in a greasy mechanic rag behind the
        hydraulic lifts in a gas station
because the gas attendant sees your skirt lifted way up to that
        triangle
        of white pink panty splotch
        and when washing those undergarments
like a man's got shit stains on his shorts
        you got them white-cream dried lip marks from juicing
        stir-crazy in your seat wanting some cock

it just doesn't make sense
    us sexes
    ho-haaing
    each other like saints holding rocks and the first to run and
        break
from the line
    gets splat
    to a mushy gnat under the thumb of so many righteous
        women and men.
    Still there's nobody talking about
how we grew to be
    so woman-hating.
We have mythology mask books on coffee tables
    men crooning Eastern chants and holding hands to let the
        agony
well out and fly
on tattered wings
    all these upper-class ins and outs for dealing with hate
but what about us blues men
    yeowl'd on whiskey-runners' moonshine
    who haven't got a lizard's lick of respect
for them soul-hocking cotton-heart-stuffed healing idols
    in truth
limp-dicked neutered trust-fund wimps
    is how I hear they are
    broken reeds in the harmonica . . .

    This here is an education.
    Remember when you felt your first piece?
    Remember when your mother threw her Kotex in the
        wastebasket?
    Remember when you first felt a girl's tongue in your mouth
    remember your first hard-on
    remember when you first came
    cherry blood not smelling so good as you imagined the oasis
        to be

her hair all askew and makeup smeared
you pretending love
whispered sweet lasagna
in her ear
at the first dance
at the first date
at the first meeting on the lawn at night
or in the basement
or when her parents were gone and you got your shorts all wet
or when you and other guys banged her in the butt
remember that
now with BA MA PhD
no memory
no flashbulb, it's burnt
from too many conferences with colleagues
no one remembers nothing
except I'm here to tell you what I heard and saw
twanging these blues on the porch step
I remember
how men's mouths were bear traps gnawing pretty ankles
and right now the male in me
yearns mutely, wanting to know how to talk again
right now the male in me seeks a road to tell my feelings
back to the lost way
other half of myself
is dying and has been wrenched and torn from his good loving side
his other half
wants to prove he's not lonely not sensitive
but if you could hear him howl now
it's the howl of a person cut in half
the howl
alone and despairing, ugly and rich with desolation
even the cruelest critics
with grenades in each hand and climbing Jack's beanstalk close to
heaven
would hold their ears with their hands

because it is such a human cry
          such a human cry of hurt and remorse and love and compassion
          so unreal
          and so earthen . . .

Eight

Sex goes deep in me
          drums with Mayan beat
          I feel sex heat in me
sex goes deep in me
          ancient as fire
          human beings learned to use
I say it goes deep in me
          and rises from my stomach to my heart
          as the sun rises on the horizon at dawn
it goes as deep in me
          as the first Mayan chiseled stone
          a mason placed as the corner stone
          for the first temple
deep in me
          before the rains died
          when oceans evaporated
deep in me
          at the beginning of human species
now not a taint of sexuality
          in the violin
          or guitar
          or literature
          or relationships
at dances, everybody staring, ready to fight
          butter-tongued and nodding of hats
          tweed-coat greetings with thumbs-up smiles.

                    *   *   *

We violate ourselves
        get up looking at this woman next to you
        wishing she were
a thousand miles away
        a thousand times different than she is
        astonished you made such a mistake long ago
thinking lust was love
walking hand in hand down a dark rained-on street
        talking young talk and family and future
never believing for a minute you'd
grow to hate her
        little by little, spider crawling on your sleeping lips
        biting you, you awake with a red mark on your lower lip
slowly venom spreads in your words and actions
        toward the one you used to love.
That's violation.
        Some say it's not natural to stay with one female
I know men who have a different woman every meal
        every day
        every year
switching suited somber priest-types with pipes
        they're a little more honest
that those Stetson gray-hatted ones
        redneck cologne sticking bits of tissue
        to their nicked chins
        properly clutching their wife's hand
or them other ones working for the government tax departments
        lighthearted polka waltzers at home
        and at work with all the young secretaries
        fire and smoke in the straw
work-worn dicks and jackal appetites
        beneath their cleaner-pressed suits
        dicks as red and raw as the eyes of mourners
        their wives are
successful types
        priestly and authoritative at home
        become saloon-gartered guffawing whiskeyed hussies

over lunch
while the quiet religious homemaker
sews pants and shirts and irons and prepares supper.
    I've seen your husbands
    develop from skinny hollow-cheeked knock-kneed schoolboys
with freckles and red hair
    turn to grungy warlocks
    training paratroopers to leap from planes into jungles
other men with razors hidden in their hair
poison darts beneath their tongues
get massages in hot tubs and body therapy
    dying to be tied up and whipped
the list is interminable
    as man gets tired of smelling the same old woman next him
    of seeing the corns on her toes
    of seeing her dresses in the closet
    of seeing her makeup in the bathroom
    of seeing her rise each morning next to him
tired and worn
seeing deeper into him
seeing he's not what she first thought
    that gladiator knight on a white horse
    beneath the armor was a disgruntled runt with dirty socks
        and dirty
underwear
    same old words and irks and quirks
    his cock wanting to sleep in her
not listening to her anymore
his inattention and anger rubs her wrong
    a whip on a tongue
she wishes she could
    take a knife and stab him
for not listening to her
and not being who she thought he could be when she met him.

I abhor violence
    so much

my whole body quivers with fear at violence
can't stand to see a woman hit
can't bear to see a woman slap a man
I cringe when people lose their tempers and go into
        maddening rages
hands fly at each other like black bats for the neck
    fingernails become fangs
and instead of vows to keep and nourish each other
    vows are made to kill and destroy
can't stand violence toward another human being
    for any reason.
    Why a woman and man would stand
    before a priest or justice of the peace
and say what they say
    when we all know it isn't true
    I don't rightly understand
    when we know time
time
    time's going to give each of them kicks and slaps
soon the woman's going to be licking her wounds
man's going to be taking pills to settle his stomach
    both are going to petrify and putrify
shit-souled
    burnt out
he burns what she loves
she burns what he cherishes
    burn baby
    as it's been said before.

Nine

We all spring up out of black earth of Latin America or Africa
    from One Mother
and somewhere we lost our loving side, our beads and paints and

feathers
　　and roots and songs and dances
　　and we imagined ourselves
into a piece of iron, unsheathing machine to kill and overpower
　　and oppress
　　we trampled our flower hearts
　　under iron, bloody heels and hooves and tank and jet wings
we destroyed
　　our men's temples and men's meeting places
　　where we sang and talked and cooked and laughed and
　　hugged
we destroyed those temples somewhere
　　I know
and I want 'em back
　　and I want to sing again about me
　　dancing the whole night around fire
　　under full moon into full sun.
Every time I hear some good blues
　　or some Sureño song
　　accordion and violin wake up in me
the dark cry
　　to dance to the music
parts of me
　　wake up holy-eyed blackbird-early
　　when I see a woman painted up
I remember
I painted my primal face
　　braided my black hair
　　and I hummed beneath the stars at night
it was back when
　　bloodletting was moon ritual
　　was coming out of men
　　blood coming out of men between the legs
　　the way blood from a woman comes out
men's monthly periods
　　ritualized our birthing
　　joy at being alive and walking earth.

I remember rituals of men
        lying prone on the ground
        gyrating hips and penis into First Mother
        and singing our crops tall
        and seeds to open
lines of men
        with feathers in long hair
        with paint on faces and arms and legs
lying prone facedown
        burrowing penises into little holes in the dirt we dug
        swiveling hips
        howling to earth deep inside the ground to hear us
        and create.
All the birds flew low over fields
        heavy brooding clouds black with thunder, parted for
                sunlight
        and it rained
on the fields
        we were working our creative magic back then
        we were high-jinksing
        them gambling gods
and goddesses
        to smile at our uplifted hands
        we were shedding blood flowers
drops of blood
in a gourd
        from our fingers and tongues we pricked
        every man and boy-child
dropped a tear of blood in the gourd
        and we poured whole male blood at the root of this big tree
at the roots of cornstalks
        at the roots of things we couldn't see, all the while singing
        and throwing our words like cornmeal to the wind.
We were full men
        and we're coming back
        and the coming back is hard
men in the emergency rooms on weekends

trying to nourish their lives
all confused
and women
        terribly hurt and abused.
I see
        men and women
        with fingers shot off, throats slashed, drugged up and
                beered down
        trying to find their way back to wholeness
        and they don't have money
        to interface in counseling groups
        they go to bars and bulldog each other
they weep and rage and curse and fight and shoot and laugh
        all trying to get back to the ways
        of Our First Lord Mother
every hand has a rock to throw now
every foot has a path away from home now
every tongue is iron still and dark.

Ten

        I've been inventing you for a long time
just the position I want in mind
        your face pleasing and submissive to my every regard
you laid back and on me
        in my mind.
I've been taking you further and further away from who you
        really are
and I've been treating you, treating every woman like the woman
        in my mind
the flesh-and-bone ones aren't real anymore
only the one in my mind
        she does what I want, she never speaks, she only opens and
                eases

my body on hers
      and likes what I do, which is only to love physically and
            love
more physically
      but it's all make-believe.

All my life, women have been make-believe
they've been flashes in my mind when my dick swells up and
      needs emptying
a woman appears to take the need away
      a woman appears not talking like real ones
      a woman appears and lies down in my mind
instant gratification
      instantly create a woman according to my needs, not hers
real ones have needs they have feelings they have hearts and lives
      and are human beings
but my mind-woman,
      I create her and she dissolves in the ooze of my semen
            coming
until the next time I need her
      there is no argument
      no threat
      no sense of my safety being attacked
there is only this unreal woman I have made up to take the place of
      real women.

Eleven

Sometimes there is a lust in me to be close to woman
no degrading, no loss of self-esteem
      bone-cum
      secretions
fill marrow of all my bones

        her eye light
        pierces my male insides
her smile
        curls up in me
        birthing fierce needs
        to rub against her
        to hold her on earth
        almost flying
        gathering our hands like gates that close
        out the world
and we become naked primal hungering
                animal flame of terrible delight
this need
        is part of me and you as water to thirst
        is us
        broke-loose wave, entering your darkness
        and you, mine, we become
        dark grinding dark igniting first spark
and you can think of a million reasons
        why you don't want me
        what's wrong with me
        but the fact is we are man and woman
        we sniff dark remembrances
        in each other's flesh
the dusty beginning in caves
we smell it in us
        no matter how many new clothes and conveniences you buy
we are
        human beings
        you woman
        me man
                you wo me man.

But there's a sickness in me, a real bad case of not knowing how
        to love
        or surrender myself
        to another person

to give myself up trustingly
    I can't.
    I thrust forward, then retreat and the grief is mine
I recoil from the kindness
    I place boundaries between you and me
living to get by gets in the way
    always a dead-end road, there's a crash, somebody's dead
        because love
isn't as real as hurt
    hurt is too real
    you see growing to be a man
I lost my gentleness
    no room for it in me
    I was trying real hard to be a man
    alone
and now I want to rediscover the tender side of me
    cultivate my nurturing side
    the wholeness of me.
    I want my masculinity to open in me and give life
but there's something deep in me afraid of giving up
    into your hands
    letting you stroke me
    letting you drink me in
I may never come back
    you're stealing something from me
    whatever magic you're doing to me
    makes me crazy and I'd go mad
be terribly alone again
    but I want to give it up
    tired of showing only certainty
    only strength
    only sureness
I want to hesitate, wait, nourish the emptiness
    I want to lie down and sleep the sleep of an infant again
    the smell of your womb on my skin
my heartbeat the purring rumbling of your blood pulse
    in my ears

your blood running through me
your breath breathing in me
I want to lie down like that again
but there's too much terror of you in me
too much condemnation
fear of your anger
you could do so much to me.
I am struggling to learn how to treat you
fighting with my heart now
feel it stretch and shrink
as if being hit and hit hard by you
I am bewildered
and life isn't living if we're just going to be silent
life isn't worth living—
sometimes I want you to take me down
to be aggressive
burst your feminine love on me
full sap
into me
but I'm afraid of you
so full of manly strength
inside
teach me slowly
to surrender myself
to the water-pool of your heart
I'll float on
full of violence letting go
surrendering
so much fear, so much refusal, so much terror
teach me how to touch your body
tell me a story about us walking in the park
I'll caress your nude body, we both lie nude on the grass
love, you tell me a story
while my fingers sleep on your breasts
I become mortal
filled with death
animal growl in my fingers

burn with the instinct of teeth
my hands listen to your breathing
to your deep cunt grunt
       moon language earth breaking for seed
       as we make love.
I want to wear my maleness
       wounded and human
       the way women wear their bodies
I want to be the bell in the leaves
       gracefully sounding my character
       songs of pain
leap from the frozen darkness with a thundering stun of solid notes
       from deep loneliness
go out into the world again as I truly am
       and listen to my body.

       But you see, I've been contorting myself worse than Houdini
hurting myself worse then Knievel on his motorcycle
       trying to deny everything soft from my life
denying I am as good a parent as a woman
       turn that lie to cold cadaver you can munch with your
             orange juice
       because it isn't true.
I cook and clean house and change diapers and spend hours
       every day
       with my kids.
       I understand my children's cries at night and I get up
       I console them
I don't feel odd
       I have a right to show my gentleness
       to show I love hard and mean and right
to be me for the loving
       to break the boundaries, the chain, the concertina wire
       the armed guards
       I did break through all of them
wondering who started the dividing line, the boundaries, the borders
       the chrome-plated boundaries

the sharks'-teeth boundary
that mangle and maul a man and woman relationship . . .

        I am cyclical man
        fostering-growth man—
there've been nights I was so hungry for someone to talk with,
        o, I just wanted to talk
about being a man
        sit and weave cotton quietly
and believe
        I cry
        I nurture my children
        my love is strong
I show it
        to the children holding their hands
I'm sensitive
        and giving of myself
        and it's my right
and I'm taking it
        not asking for permission
        not listening to reams of madness
what I can and can't do
        I'm me and I'm doing it, yeah! I'm doing it!

Twelve

You want me to play John Wayne
        fast-drawing on Mexican backs
        twelve-knuckling bar-hooting drunks
go ahead
but you're not going to make my children think you're a man
just a ten-gallon ugly fool
        whose mama never gave a lick of love
        if you want to express your love

face turns red, fingers start jerking for trigger and you mad-eye
        the gun cabinet
jerk your finger on yourself
        because you're not going to make my daughters believe
        a gun is the measure of a man's manhood
        because you're a fool who lacks the courage
        to speak about loneliness and confusion
and found the .44 Magnum
softer and safer than a child's hand
        makes you twice the fool
and I'm laughing at your burly cockeyed engine-gunning heart
        at your cartoon every-morning farce of what you think a
                man is
        don't believe you're alone, man
        women out there bolster you like holster to their hip
they supply the edge of proof
that you do go gunning
you're a man
        and damn if you're not a gunpowder-blowing fool
        on destruction.

        Which is another thing.
        A man is supposed to be strong, supposed to chop down
                forests
set step on new horizons
bullshit—
        men I know are too busy paying mortgages
        paying child-support payments
and never getting to see the children.
        A woman says she's got a right to abortion without his say
        what about his say-so
        they say he doesn't have a right
        and the judge says he can't be as good a parent
        and you believe that, you believe
        a banjo is a baby grand
        and it's ignorance that keeps
a man thinking he has no rights

except to kill himself
on being a man
full of shame
kill himself
for hiding his feelings
full of shame
for feeling too much
for having a heart
kill a man
for taking no more bullshit talk about how men are mute
courtiers
living in a message-note world
kill a man
for being tough, mean, just a downright man
and we have to holler it isn't true
it isn't true
been slammed down in prisons
been stripped to my shivering soul
seen the feminine part of my soul
seen in men's faces the reflection of earth springtime
seen in their eyes the softest blossoms and in their hands hardest
calluses
seen in their courage deep fear and timidity
gone out to sleep with hoboes in industrial condemned
warehouses
wart-looking men
and heard them talk the babiest talk in remorseful grief
about leaving children behind
men broken down to crumbling crackers
so don't tell me how men are so callous and dumb
fit only to cannibalize
just we are pretty confused
getting all the wrong information
both sides
both sides.

*   *   *

Loveliest woman leaning in sea-swept breeze
        on a porch gazing out on the Atlantic
sees me
rising from the sea bringing in fish and shimmering every
        stomach muscle
                bicep and thigh
        and then later, after I cut and cook the fish
        I am cooing
        my infant
        in my burly arms
        to rock asleep
many a night
        I pace my living room singing and humming like a big fat mama
        proud and feeling full of my manhood
while I sing my male gospel rancher spells
        and my infant gets all clovery green with dream
        she found in my notes
        she plucked a clover
and wished on more of Daddy's love
        and we can go on with this poem
        but my girls just got back from school
arms spread wide
full of warm nonsense words and giggly hugs
        squirming under my hell-la-shish loving hands.

Thirteen

I have to remember
        because you're ready to dismember
yeah, you just go ahead
        but I'm going to head this problem full on
        because what if our children come up
hating women

if we don't break this learning to hate ourselves
to hate women
        to hate everything
        you think children aren't going to hurt and hate
you see
        we have to talk us and women
        you see
we're both equal human beings
        shouldn't hide lust or love behind a book
        or a beard or eyeglasses or manners
don't want to hide me
my lust is good,
        could stick your hands into me up to the elbows and never feel
so sweet a goose down on your flesh, woman.
        O, my heart perches eagled on your arm
and I surrender myself to you, woman
        the way land surrenders to high tide
        or winter wool to winter wind
I do
        and more, woman
        my desire to come close to you
is sap-strong bark and cornstalk green
        jointed along the length of our years loving each other
        and I would love to know that you know that way
letting me become more of who I am,
        become more of me, I grow on growing me
        emptying our mouths of the silhouettes
        behind each word
        emptying our bodies of the pain
        all weapons
        we pile in the middle between us
        the way soldiers surrender their rifles
        to the resistance.
I wonder how our love could have crumbled.
        Remember the first way I made love the way you liked:
        a light summer sun-shower
        opening the flower seed.

But over the years
        the rain passed through climatic changes and turned to hail:
the horses in the field tried to shield themselves from it
they turned right, then left, while each
        tried to get in front of the other
        to shield themselves from the burning hail
        with no way out
        the pain bent their forelegs and they collapsed
        in the dust.
Both our hearts cringe, twitch, seek escape
and then lie down like that.
        Perhaps it is body memory
        how I remember my hands gripping Mother's thighs
        suckling at her breast
        entangled in her hair
        clutching her constantly
                and how
my body seeks that connection with you.

Now at the window, where I saw the horses go down
        I watch you drive away
angrily, gravel seethes from your spinning tires
        and the umbilical cord snaps.
        The horses went down
        pitilessly at the mercy
        of hail.
Your blue car turns at the stop sign
        and then you're gone.

        Horses were under siege
        tried to fight hail off
        tried to flee
        finally
                capitulated.
        Their surrender so human
        so much strength and dignity
        in the quavering flanks

in those front legs bending
the dark crevice of the knees
finally giving up all hope
I saw us.

In the garden behind the house, hail shredded the flowers.
But the first year—
    I didn't mind
    cropping vegetable leaves in the garden until my knees bled
    nor stuccoing walls in March wind until my chapped lips
        cracked and bled
    nor building the adobe fence until my hands bled
I gave thanks
for our life together.

All winter I have been coughing and sleeplessly fighting off
    bronchial asthma.
I used to love you, woman
    the way a wolf's tongue thrusts up to catch blue-bodied
        raindrops
    my tongue darted in you.
    We lay in bed and I softly bit your flesh
    a jaguar cub gnawing the steel spindles of his zoo cage.
This has been a particularly hard year for us
friends, wines and books bring little reprieve.
When a coyote howls his male-need call for his mate
with tensile gait, loping buoyantly at the crest of sand dunes,
    profiled against moon
I see her come
    and I want to howl for you
    but instead I curse—
    what the fuck you want me to do!
    I don't need this shit from you!
O, but I remember the first year
a thousand bees filled
my fingertips with spring
when I touched you

and your nipples were pomegranate seeds
and all summer my lips were red,
your laughter oceaned out
and freed the nets in me
and our bodies moved as wind pushed flames
through brittle grass toward each other!

But what has happened?
I clench my knuckles
    and I want to leave.
We have not held each other warmly in a long time.
This has been a homeless winter.
It has been a bad winter for us.
    I want to leave
    my house, my beliefs, my gods
    and you
    and become someone else
    in another place and time.
Our teeth are serrated links
of handcuffs
snapping curses to hiss the other shut.
Ice between us cracks, and you cry
and my fear suspends itself from a rib hook
freezing meat in an icehouse.
I pray the ice will hold
to carry me across to a bar
where over whiskey shots
I can complain to another man:
    Man, I try to make her happy—I quit
    trying last night—I turned
    and spit out "fuck you!"
    Accuse me of being insensitive
    of never fulfilling you
    of raping you emotionally
    of not knowing how to make love
    well, the hell with that bullshit!

              ✷   ✷   ✷

But I didn't do this male ritual
instead
clouds part out the window and moonlight
spreads on my part of the bed. I stare
at the moon and I can't reach over
and touch you, woman
can't kiss you
can't hold you
can't make love
because my touch draws pain from you
the way a rose picker's hand
brings in only barbs
from green stems.
                    Yes, the horses fell
                          and hail shredded the flowers.
These days of hate
play themselves out
a needle that skids across the album
scratching a new song across the old song
of how you hate my hands
hate my eyes
hate my voice
hate my feelings
hate me
hate men.

And after days of hate
        what do we do?
Make love on the floor
my heart sings to the predawn color of your skin
old bells on Andean Peaks in so much solitude and silence
        beating
        I am alive I am alive I am alive
to all the earth and sky
        bells sound in my male dance blood
        I am alive.

                    *   *   *

But Grandma taught me when I was a boy how to suck poison
        from a snake bite:
Chew the skin good, chew well, then suck and spit, mijito
increase the hurt, widen the pain
        taste the pain
        the hurt
        touch the darkness
        see and feel the poison in all life
        it is the dark work of life.
Go down into the wound
work your healing by entering the pain
then spit out the poison.

This love is a fish hook
        in my thumb
        can't pull out the barb
        on the other end
        the eye
so I scrape around the hook
in my thumb with my pocketknife blade
widen the hole, increase the pain
all of myself uttered in pain
as I cut the hole rounder
wound blood pours and what I am made of
hurts, I dig deeper and deeper
        work my healing
        then
        extract the hook, clean the wound
        and have learned about myself.

        Men are returning home
        rising
        from their dying
        to live over again
        with their children
men are returning to their children

                        ✳   ✳   ✳

I fix my daughters' swing set, tighten screws on the slide
change diapers sitting on the toilet
      while my other daughter stands in doorway
      next in line on my lap
I move and they follow
I cook and they eat
I sleep and they wake
I sing a new man to them
      they stand in my male shade, I purr my jaguar growl
      they crouch and grunt and leap at my chest
my hands are ripe fruit they nibble
      I sniff
they paw
      we skip and leap across the living room, dancing, yelling
healing myself
      we hug, wrestle
      spin and jump and scamper and land on all fours
      on the carpet
      my children leap and laugh with me
      in our male song, Ahoa, Grandfather!
      Ahoa! Grandmother!

Book V

Rebirth

One

A cremation, my own, each day
   I awake from a charred dream world
in a blaze of birds singing out my bedroom window,
  the flat, hollowed stone of my heart
   I grind dreams in, to ground meal, and scatter over thirty years
of my life—
to the birds I give—
   what else is there?
   Those tunnels of people I knew and held my courage
    up, torched
their shadows with my fearful face, to know their darkness
is how I have lived, always in the darkness, always ignorant,
always making choices that will benefit the children of the earth.

What else is there?
We are extinct and live in ruins
  unless
    we claim our courage to praise each day,
try to be brothers all in all,
sisters all in all,
like sea waves overlapping, rushing, high whitecap arcing, rearing
  madly
at what hurts us, to live
     peacefully . . .
I proudly wear the whip wounds
given me by men I have spat at, refused to let ride me.
Think of the leaf as a supernatural being,
  go to the hills and become a cave dweller
then come back and tell me

who you are.
We will be one, earthenware that carries the water
to children thirsty for life,
hand-shaping their lives like water shapes the seed open
        into its own self.

Two

        Came the birthing hour of delight
        of being myself
        gestation into clarity out of squalor
        I came out from the blue prisons of my language
        from the ravaged gates of my words
        into the red hour of my freedom
        epicenter of earthquaked me
        afraid to speak, yet I reel in flight
        a low-flying crane risking the shotguns of hunters below
        risking the jowls of hounds
        carrying me to their powerfully jawed owners' cages . . .

I am here with my grief and body songs
my loving self urged to trace its earthquaked origins
I give my eyes to you to throw the brown stones out to sea again
I give you my broken-backed heart, a twisted mass of rock
I've carved into gates of hell and entered
I give you my happiness, a woven cord stretched
taut against the soul
that holds itself against desert-blowing sands
the happiness I step out of each day into a world of ice
I thaw out.

How these words barely skim the surface
of where I have been and been through.
Each road I take has me arriving at the same crossroads

the bulky-brawned cottonwood languishes in deep
solace of summer's unwavering gaze
and the colt bounds away on lightning hooves
each hoof strident as a sculptor's chisel
cracks against rock, all things are so filled with life
I wish I could name one image to convey
my inexorable love of life!

But human joy spreads itself into a lifetime
and we cannot
point to any one thing
and say this is what life meant and this is what I felt
instead a whole life describes one moment
and one indescribable moment is described by the whole life.
I drive my truck to my cabin.
My sadness
hibernates in me brooding salmon in my blood
at the edge of my face, gloom glides on updrafts of my breath—
I am an old mountain lion
dragging the rotten carcass of his habits to his lair.
But I sing my regeneration now
my voice does not have
distance in it of the parade horse bedecked in silver reins
dawdling bally-whoa whinnies
nor is my hand the manicured
conqueror's hand forcing others to kiss the ring
instead
I kiss my child's head and speak my feelings close to my heart
I have walked away from the slush-fund hustlers groggily
yawning favored mouths to consume
and consume and I have returned
to work the ground and plant trees and teach the children how to
read and write—
I have changed, turning from hard-fisted
disciplinarians and twittering speech givers, from handshaking
crowd dazzlers
from the clappers and whistlers to become silent

again in my own solitude
where I can expose the lies in me
and cut away the threads
and see my interior design, the underside
of the wound. It is much more. I am tired of all the fanfare
and false promise
the empty praise and the generous sanctification
heaped on King Death Makers
from senators to celebrities to common folk . . .

I want to return to living with simple dignity,
not a life of crystalline goblets brimming with wine
Super Bowl tickets and Costa Rican vacations
I want to sit on the
plank bench in the backyard
of a friend in the barrio and hear
the story of how he came up with a goat for the Fourth of July:

Pues, *me and some* vatos *got into our* ranfla, *each of us had*
bats ese, *and we crawled into Bush's field on our bellies,*
fijate, wachate, *the watchman had his trailer door open and*
still ese, *we hit the goats with our bats and dragged them to*
our car while he was shooting at us—man, the whole barrio
had goat meat to eat, all the niños *and* viejas y viejos, *simon*
ese, *we were shooting our guns and exploding fireworks and no one*
was poor that day carnal, ninguno faltaba carnal . . .
and instead of posing with a stolid shield face
I want to cry until my ears
        and nose and eyes are puffy red from crying
yeah,
I've changed from a museum Chicano to a goat-stealing barbecuing
        vato
from a professor chairing a VIP round-table committee
to a poet working with kids in the barrio boxing gym
and open my cherry-box heart and give each child a chocolate poem.

                    *   *   *

I've been hooed and jeered at because I refused to
              conjure up
lies about our pious attitudes toward our bodies
my heart is a paper bag carrying bread
not a soap-bubble machine spewing roseate bubbles up marble
              stairs—
I am trying to say I have changed and I celebrate my change
and I no longer adjust my
                            life to fit your entry and exit
no doorman here shimmying my
life to close quietly and open easy
                      I am strange and hesitant
proud to have survived
and I don't carry a business card to mark my wolf territory
no portfolio or ID except my poems.

But it's not even that—what I am trying to say is that
I've crawled out of the smashed wreckage of my life alive
in a crazy living way
death made each of my steps upward
take me deeper down to seeing myself
how odd I should still be here
trying to put myself back together
and that I am makes me want to
sing and tell the world how afraid I was
to speak the truth
to claim myself a poet
shaking my weed-stick as a conductor for the breeze
blowing through the leaves and how the
dust applauded me on barren bleak afternoons
when I walked all alone
and passed houses where I could hear someone playing a piano inside
and Lord how I dreamed of playing music one day!
How I bowed in make-believe festivals with rocks and water and
       wind and sunshine
and jowl-slavering mutts, how I invented my
mumble boogy-joogy ayy-no man-sighings

and romped in my pompous oratories
how I was king of the anthill prophesying to stray
dogs how the world would love me wrapped in a gunnysack cape
I somberly intoned the rules of my childhood games to all
inhabitants of the prairie
and all of it out of pure love for
life and people.

And that is not it either—I have changed and healed myself
I see stragglers of homeless, bundled soiled
belongings on their backs
I remember my childhood homelessness
chavlito on my wheela burn-marking sidewalks with my signature
popping brodies off curbs whistling my Indio whistle
I turned in the world like the spokes of my chromed rims turned in
silver flashes, minutes blazed up in fire and flame
my broken street life dragging like a muffler pipe
I gripped my handlebars and spun and raced and leaped with no
        message except joy
at being alive . . .

Booked for things I didn't do
playing dominoes on D-home bunks
banging the cell bars with my broomstick
my Bach, my window of the world
I said no to the raw and bloody world
I screamed against it all
I turned away from it
until I had no scream left
one had to turn mean one had to get drunk one had to destroy
        oneself
as much as possible and still live to do it
again the next day
a mule for the beating board I was
and now there's been a change come about
I feel I've descended on a refuge lake

that leafed laughter in me as I glide softly down
to a place I've been longing for, blue heron man-hard for
others to take me down, I glide on my own and stand on the
        place
I choose—but even that's not describing this change in me.

Three

Sun at my back
into the evening I go
on the freeway
wanting another world

thinking of friends
words we've spoken and stories told
in front yards and kitchens
when we drank wine
and sensed another season coming
when each had things to do again,
then I would leave,
do something I've never done before,

trade sunlight for shadows
streams and woods for the highway,
the warm smiles of folks
who have grown to know me
for the grimace of a stranger
whose words betray my trust,
I trade the hours I could have stayed
and was welcomed
for hours that unfold their terror
in hotel rooms,
I trade intimacy for airport crowds

and traffic mazes,
I trade the hands that gave to me
for ones that steal from me,
warm company for distant acquaintances,
magical love for the magic of drugs,
I give myself away and feel a great emptiness

feel a darkness in life
that builds itself around me
and with sun in my face
I take the freeway
meet the dawn and bargain for my meaning
with meaninglessness,
trade myself away for the emptiness
of faces at truck stops,
in another beginning, in another city,
in another change, I gleam and darken
with the blown light of freedom
streaking through me
to a beginning
to the darkness
and disorder.

The curves of mountain roads,
dry flatlands and red clay banks
growing me new again—
I multiply myself
to a hundred voices and faces
to meet what
will come
and in all of them, find myself.

Four

      I must call back that part of me
           extinct as the peregrine falcon was.
If I held out my arms in the field
and stood there
swinging the bloody chunks of my soul around
on a length of leather
would it circling high out of sight see me
with its sharp brown eye
and dive toward my arm . . .
      It does not trust me anymore.
      It does not know me.
If that part of me is listening tonight
I am here for you
      that part
      I opened hunting season on
if you hear, falcon soul,
please return to me.
      I am preparing my body for you
      a nest.
I am going searching for you
waiting patiently on the mesa.

      How does one persuade that part of oneself
      to return—
      that part that spoke the truth, that found peace
      and beauty and meaning in each day . . .
I have no idea.
Except to climb back into the rubble of myself every day
go over again the days I've lived since your departure
and stand fast in the farthest reaches of myself

those prison days in my cell
those lonely days as a teenager when I was the only
        one roaming
ditches
I must go back to.

That whirring at the ear I sometimes hear
a hummingbird's wings
that slightly flurry air to breeze at my ear
is my falcon self
skimming over me.

And where do our spirits go when we maim them
with our poisons?
This falcon flew from my fingertips
when it smelled fighting blood on them
it screeched a maddening shriek
from my clutch when it saw me
        disrespecting it.

        I tied a hood cowl over its eyes
        so it wouldn't see what I was doing to my body
        to my heart
        and placed it in the cage of my brain.
Staggering in fields
I went and lived
instead of seeing its graceful flight
its terrible dive on prey
        I tore out its claws
        I singed its feathers
        destroyed its nest
        blinded it
        grounded it in a cage

and one night after abusing myself, I awoke
        and found the cage open
        found blood spots on my hands

scratches on my face
and knew Spirit Falcon freed itself
from seeing
from being
in me
choking on smoke from crack
it left me an empty cage.

I do not think the good man is extinct.
If I am truthful and honorable
and live with integrity
on a morning walk in the future
I will place my hands to shade my eyes
from the sun
        and see it circling again above me
        and I will let my arm out,
        it will dive down in majestic roar
        of feathers
        and sit on my forearm
        talons tight around my flesh
        then
fly into my mouth
and I will surrender to it
what I have been keeping in promise
a good healthy life
a respect for truth.

        I feel wind on my face
and remember my flight . . .
O Peregrine Falcon
loosen your wings again
in the green depths of my soul
in the vast gorges that have formed
with blue shimmering
light awaiting your return

        I await.

Five

This November day . . . the cold the last few days
has broken all records in the East and Midwest. On the
    six o'clock news
I see people, dark-coated shadows leaning forward in gray sheets
    of snow.
But this hard harsh cold
hurts me with its beauty. The air is like a woman I read of once,
in a Russian novel, a beautiful dark-haired woman
with cold red cheeks and lips, who, before entering her carriage,
stopped on the marble steps of her palace to look at me for an
    instant.
I knew she loved me. And then went away. This kind of hurt,
I feel, the numb love
of a man in reverie over the fallen leaves. Each bronze-brown leaf
is a *santuario.* Through its wrinkled, curled husk,
evening sun radiates as if it were the silent, somber hallways of a
    mountain
church. The veins of the leaf remind me of the old pictures
that decorate ancient altars—Our Lady of Guadalupe,
robed in reds and blues, peeling, withering colors,
the earth, wind, water and sun painted like four Chicanos,
the unbroken tribe, carving from inside of the trunk, a delightful
effigy of the only religion, the oldest religion . . . these saints
that go flying past my window, that I trample underfoot,
that I feed to the cows and horses,
that I lie under on a steel swing cot on warm afternoons and read
    poetry,
often looking up into the massive clutter of leaves in the
    cottonwood,

totally overwhelmed by their beauty, that in my heart
the eternal orb of being that I am emanates and radiates light
    with joy.
Sweet November day . . .

Six

Why does the sun
gladden me
    drumming its golden baton
    on my heart
    beckoning me to dance in the light?
Why does this overcast morning
    its clouds thinly stretched over the mesas
    with a hint of snow coming in
    remind me of a grandmother
        hanging sheets on a line?
Why am I reminded of myself as if I were
    looking into an old black-and-white photograph,
    I'm standing in front of a farmhouse
    in a plain dark suit,
        with a fedora shading my eyes?
I know that when the wind comes,
    the strong prairie breezes start blowing,
    I'll be flung like a handful of sand
    into the fallow fields,
        my dark suit coat
        caught on a broken board beside the house.
So much silence, so much distance around me,
    a lifelong of memories spattering
        like heavy rainfall
        on the parched furrows.

Seven

Stones encountered along the way.
The stones that have comforted me through my quest
have the natures of words well thought out—
stones molded by breathing centuries.
                                        I wonder
what makes a place its own. The stones by the river
are of the river, know the river, commune
with the river. And these other hoary, scarred, flake-
        encrusted stones
in the prairie are of their place.
There's been no compromise for them,
and it makes me want to curl up inside each stone
and sleep, unaware of the world beyond me,
rest . . .
        Each stone I come to carries the calm serenity
of praying hands. I would like to say
the world demands we compromise, but the stones,
those throwaway god-words, those touched by grace,
those children in the weeds and silent in their
        uncompromising world
have been for me the steady-full backups
my prayers lichen on and mote the air with grainy pleadings
of love and hope. But more that—with some people, they
        are always
praying for others' sufferings, it's always
his suffering be lessened, her suffering be lifted,
the ravaged warred-upon peaceful farmer that witnesses his
        daughter raped,
his son beheaded, while in cathedrals

the prayers float like white doves to crystalline ceiling and
	shatter their heads like birds
against a cabin's window.
Stones have that ruffled edge of being silent when asked
	a question, being sweet in the harshest
climates,
they say little and mean everything. In the same place they inhabit,
so much life is lived.
In the space they have settled in, so much
rightness of living is fostered.
My prayer to them is the hidden prairie dove I saw
while running last week, I glanced at the flick-flight of a
	prairie dove
and saw its expanding tail feathers fan
out,
revealing a white ridge tipping each feather,
it was a prayer I seek as a lining to each night when I fall asleep.
For the stone, I believe, prayer
	is the essential component to its being.
O Great Creator, let honesty and truth
fill me, attend me, weigh me down
as stones in the mouth, stones in the hands.
I once had a friend
just out of prison who invited me
to do a sweat with him.
Entering the tepee, suspended from center lean-pine pole
a net of cactus fiber and in the net a stone,
hanging just above the hot lava rocks
steaming.
He said to me, *I have so much hate and hurt that my*
	heart is the stone
and as long as it takes
for the fire, heat and steam to wear this rock down
to a pebble,
I will come and pray for prayer to wear down my hatred for them,
for what they've done, the sorrow for what I've done to myself,
to others, to existence.

I will always be here, reckoning me down a single prayer
repeated until I am dust.
When I walked out into the bright sunshine, got back in my truck
        and drove off,
doves with white fringed tails were flying from my fingertips
out the driver's window into the open blue sky—
                I felt like a surface
                where hunters cut open birds and gut innards,
                felt opened by a blade's parched hunger
to be honest with myself.
Now, in my forty-fifth year on earth, I will visit the stones again,
        this afternoon,
        and pray.

Eight

I wake up
and walk down to the lake and pray
with patience, thanking the water
the trees and mist-smoldering earth.
To speak the truth in all I say,
direct my sights on the vision of fulfilling
my dream
        to live clean and sober and truthful
with elegance of the dark sprig
                unbudded, peacefully embracing the cold
hours, welcoming the warmth,
        always with my face toward the sky,
embalmed and overwhelmed in fragrance of wild love
for all life,
        to stay steady and grip the course
with surefooted heartful groundedness,
never again allow myself to succumb to foul misery
of self-loathing, never forget the past

but make the present and future a cavalry horn blasting
at dawn that nothing will stop me from going forward
to face the enemies, reach for the wounded,
enter into the woods that call me to sing
to become the vision of the dream
      to become a pure person in thought and deed,
      and for this I pray to God and the Great Creator
      that I am given the strength and love for myself
to endure the dark moments, the hellish temptations
that want to destroy my songs and silence my dream,
may I weep when I hurt,
share my love when I love,
be there when I am called upon,
may I not waver from my duty as a poet
      to sing
         so strong, that if I utter a vowel in the valley,
         mountain-peak pine needles will shiver with joy.
      May I reclaim my soul through such efforts,
         may I show my real face to the sun
         and my deepest pain to the evening
         that the day has to end.
      I bring my soul to you, o world, as one
         might steal a flower from a neighbor's garden
         as an offering
         to his love waiting at her parents' bedroom window.

Nine

It was the quiet moments standing at the bank
studying the water
emptying my mind of work, obligations,
lawyers, payments,
      that made the silence that much sweeter,
      knowing I'd returned like a small boy

back home,
>> a bowl of stew on the table
>> and loving arms to tuck me in.

It was the sound of the creek roar
and cottonwood leaves rustling and breeze through grasses
that made me lift my head to the sky
and sing sounds I recall I might've made
when I was a wild boy.

Ten

If it does not feed the fire
of your creativity, then leave it.
If people and things do not
inspire your heart to dream,
then leave them.
If you are not crazily in love
and making a stupid fool of yourself,
then step closer to the edge
of your heart and climb
where you've been forbidden to go.
Debts, accusations, assaults by enemies
mean nothing,
go where the fire feeds you.
Turn your attention to the magic of whores,
grief, addicts and drunks, until you stumble upon
that shining halo surrounding your heart
that will allow you to violate every fear happily,
be where you're not supposed to be,
the love of an angel who's caught your blood on fire
again, who's gulped all of you in one breath
to mix in her soul, to explode your brooding
and again, your words rush from the stones

like a river coursing down
from some motherly mountain source,
and if your life doesn't spill forth
unabashedly, recklessly, randomly
rushing in wonder at life,
then change, leave, quit, silence the idle chatter
and do away with useless acquaintances
who have forgotten how to dream,
bitch rudely in your dark mood at the mediocrity
of scholars who meddle in whimsy for academic trifles—
let you be their object of scorn,
let you be their object of mockery,
let you be their chilling symbol
of what they never had the courage to do, to complete, to follow,
let you be the flaming faith that makes them shield their eyes
as you burn from all sides,
taking a harmless topic and making of it a burning galaxy
or shooting stars in the dark of their souls,
illuminating your sadness, your aching joy for life,
your famished insistence for God and all that is creative
to attend you as a witness to your struggle,
let the useless banter and quick pleasures
belong to others, the merchants, computer analysts
and government workers;
      you haven't been afraid
      of rapture among thieves,
      bloody duels in drunken brawls,
      denying yourself
      the essence of your soul work
      as poems rusted while you scratched
      at your heart to see if it was a diamond
      and not cheap pane glass,
now, then, after returning from one more poet's journey
in the heart of the bear, the teeth of the wolf,
the legs of the wild horse,
sense what your experience tells you,
your ears ringing with deception and lies and foul tastes,

now that your memory is riddled with blank loss,
tyrants who wielded their boastful threats
to the sleeping dogs and old trees in the yards,
now that you've returned from men and women
who've abandoned their dreams and sit around
like corpses in the grave moldering with regret,
steady your heart now, my friend, with fortitude
long-lasting enduring hope, and hail the early dawn
like a ship off coast that's come for you,
spent and ragged and beggared,
if what you do and how you live does not feed the fire
in your heart and blossom into poems,
leave, quit, do not turn back,
move fast away from that which would mold your gift,
break it, disrespect it, kill it.
Guard it, nurture it, take your full-flung honorable
heart and plunge it into the fire
into the stars, into the trees, into the hearts of others
sorrow and love and restore the dream
by writing of its again-discovered wild beauty.

Eleven

I asked my daughter what I should write about
and passing me in the living room
where I was lying on the couch
she answered, *Heart.*
She didn't mean
the mass of muscles that keeps us alive
but the other heart
that dreams and thrives on meaningful relationships.
The one I see in children in Mexico
who dig a pocket-size hole in the dirt
and stand ten feet away

and toss a washer
trying to make it in the hole.
She meant the heart in my hands
when I wring out the mop in the sink
and bend to swab the kitchen floor,
the heart that bleeds thorns into her flesh
when parents quarrel and seethe with accusations,
the heart that pulsed so strong when she got
a piece of the ball
at the Little League game yesterday.
The heart that shrivels every time a drug addict
stabs a vein with a needle,
not the mass of muscle that courses blood
and oxygen through veins
but the heart that blisters on a man's hands
picking vegetables all day,
the one in the words of Cesar Chavez that broke
into a thousand pieces of bread for field-workers to eat
and dream on,
the heart that pounded in Pancho Villa's horse's hooves
when it raided a train packed with American millionaires,
the heart that wept in Cegoya's tears when assassinated,
the heart that weeps when Chicano children
go without a meal for three days
and the heart that sings to the sun
when family comes together,
when there are no more accusations, no betrayals,
when the doctor exits the operation room and smiles,
when the check arrives and you can fill the grocery basket
full of your favorite foods,
when a poem grips at the air,
a power that sings in its lines,
calling for more heart,
give us more heart in the university programs
and not the sterile computers that teach students
ambition is more important than compassion,
more heart in the bankers who decide to level a barrio

for upscale gentrified folks,
more heart in publishers who abuse their writers and poets
who cheetah-smile to win your trust
and after the manuscript is theirs,
they toss coconuts on your head
and banana peelings in your path,
she meant heart in the way a child feels
able to almost touch the stars
sitting in his first tree house.
She meant heart in the way those children
in Chiapas played with a piece of metal,
hysterically giggling when they made it in the hole,
innocent of the fact that in America
children were garage-saling toy boxes heaped
with Nintendos, TVs, bikes, bears, boats,
innocent of ambition in their parents' planning college
and saving plans and striving for headliner stardom,
the children play this moment,
in their dreams they are remembering how they chased a grasshopper
with parade hailing of laughter and excitement,
they are dreaming of a world filled with penny washers,
laughing with full hearts
when luck is theirs and one goes in.
My daughter meant heart in a way an alcoholic vows
not to drink again and an addict not to shoot up again,
heart in a way that has nothing to do with pacesetters,
that has nothing to do with the color green
and everything to do with the colors of a rainbow,
and answers questions about love and guilt and hate and hope.
She meant heart in the way the common sparrow
chirps at the illustrious coming of a new day
filled again with washers and dusty holes.

Twelve

Sunflowers—
how they love the murk-suck bottom
    of the mother ditch
to display their arm-spread enthusiasm
            for life.
    Wish I had that
as I jog the haggard gravel access road
    parallel to the ditch
I notice
there are none on the incline
            going up
but in the murk-sog and on the embankment shoulder
they wave to me. The sight of them in the clumped ooze
            and on top,
amid seed-hefty grass
bird-tracked and curling for want of rain,
    wonders me—

I think of children on the playground at recess,
without rule, each gives to the other that magic space
            needed to play
and it really is they who watch me running
trying to stay healthy, to live
to be old—
after all the drugs I've put in my body
to get blazed, blitzed, drunk—
        a drug-snorting booze-guzzling
know-it-all, defiant, gutsy street fighter fending for ways
not to live . . .

they're all here, waiting as they did when I was a kid,
welcoming me back to the beginning of another day.
        It wonders me—
seeking my renewal, I gutted drug dealers' inventory
until I was an out-of-style department-store floor-model mannequin
disposed of in the landfill of dark cantinas, recycled at the
        dealer's table,
        in near-escapes with cops chasing me, trigger-cocked thugs
            I hustled,
flipping vehicles on the roadside, passing red lights during rush
        hour—
        somehow I'm here
        in the playground of wild sunflowers,
panting hard to outrun the monarch butterfly that just passed me:
if these are the crossroads where the living meet the dead,
        I've arrived
to mourn my past, rejoice the present, hope for a better future,
with heaven and hell in each foot I put down
        to move on,
                toward the center of myself.
A county-jail guard once knocked out a tooth
smacking me across the face with his club.
I took that tooth and sharpened it on my cell floor
to an arrow head tied to my toothbrush with floss
to later stab him with it—
        I never did
        but with the same commitment I once took my brogan
        and cot leg of angle-iron
        and hammered against the bars to escape, which I did,
        hammering that boot and metal leg for months,
        I finally cut that bar they said was impossible to cut through
                with a boot and cot leg—
        it's a lesson that if I can do that,
        when it comes to the business of living,
                I can do anything.

Thirteen

Back to my body and my macaw-colored soul.
We once drew the boundaries of war
seeking to destroy each other. I abused it,
soaked it in whiskey, kept sleepless
guard over it, drenched it in drugs,
hoping to escape it.

It and I. Two of us. From the depths in me,
a blending union rises, like dew at dawn
on the leaves of my arms,
on the clover of my hair,
blending me with blue morning sky,
with the wiry flight of sandhill cranes,
with an old woman's voice down the dirt street
calling for husband, deaf and wobbling on his cane
against his front adobe wall.

I believe my body springs from the earth—
my daughter wrestles it, takes my hand
like brown water and scoops it up,
falls upon my chest in bed
as she does outside in the alfalfa,
listening to my heartbeat
as she does the vibrations of earth outside.

Inside me she imagines dark caves
where she lived before.
Outside me she sees trees reach down
their limbs under blowing winds,

and she remembers her own voice singing
in the darkness of earth's underground.

How long it has taken me to recognize
my earthiness. I have long thrown myself
to the dust, the rocks, the trees and water,
but only now am I learning
their words, reading their ways, following
them back down into my blood
where they sleep, curled like snakes
on the red-sun stone of my heart.

What am I saying? For an instant
that drew itself out
like a spark into a forest fire,
I let myself be taken by the cities' glamour,
indulging freely in whiskey
and drugs, thrusting my love upon others,
ashamed of the act, white with guilt,
I coated myself with paint
and jewels . . .
        I fell like a doll
        on the floor
        my plastic face cracked
        down through my deadly smile.

Earth, I come to you now,
in my baggy khaki pants and heavy boots,
rugged and worn, scarred and silent,
and rub a piece of ground as I would a child's head.
How odd, that you have given birth to me,
and I in turn, more wise and experienced,
have now given birth to you in me.
We blend into each other,
as do the great spaces of plains and silence;
my voice rolls from my mouth

windy and typhoonlike, spiraling its own dance
of joy.

I stop for a minute and praise the earth,
I invite all people to stop
their crackling machines and praise the earth:
come, let us praise the earth,
each in our own ways—
                          the poet
erases the borders, the housewife sweeps
racism from her front step, the bus driver
welcomes everyone on, the children
sing *Life is in the air* and the old men cry
Life is underground,
each in our own way
come, let us praise the earth!

Half of my spirit has always remained
straw and mud—
a pit I dug down below my flesh
to pray in.

My face forged from brown sand,
my body gorged out by rain,
sun shimmered light upon
the red-brown clay I was.
Earth bit into rocks
like soft bread
giving me portions
to build my shelter with.

Sun passed through me
and left its pawprint
upon the mud, which dried,
whose mold my heart formed in.

                    ✻   ✻   ✻

I shattered rosary beads—
black seeds of death
that blossomed death in my people.

I burned the cross
to cook sheep I stole from
Spanish fields
and made my club
from the blue- and brown-robed statues
I toppled from altars.

I danced in the warm ashes
of burnt churches
and shook my singing gourds,
swirled my eagle feathers,
all soaked in missionary blood.

Fourteen

       I had an incredible dream last night. I was in a Chinese marketplace. A huge, dark, dreary, threatening makeshift city where poor from all over the world descended and howled their goods for sale. It was night. I was in a small coal-mine boxcar with an old Chinese man. We were headed across a bridge when suddenly, before us, the drawbridge started to open. I became fearful. We were going to fall off. I could see faraway high-rises, millions of lit windows. The bridge slowly closed. Then I was in a crumbling tenement, the air clammy, wet and dark. I ran downstairs, cubicled with thousands of stalls and booths, and out into the streets, where on a street corner I met an old lover of mine—she was drunk, working as a prostitute to supply her heroin habit. I walked her across the street. Then woke up.
       The old iron bridge, its dark beastlike iron
          architecture, hordes

of Chinese, then the vast heavens opening up to me . . .
　　　　　rather than the bridge taking this odd Chinese man
　　　　　　　　and me over a river,
　　　　　the dream was asking me to cross
myself
　　　　　to leave the dark marketplace where flesh and lust and
　　　　　　　drugs and whiskey
　　　　　are sold to appease the struggling spirit
　　　　　to blind the eyes
　　　　　dull the touch
　　　　　cut out the tongue
　　　　　and leave one without spirit-print . . .
As the bridge drew itself wide, opening to the vast brilliance of
　　　night stars,
it was my own invented self yawning its jaws.
　　　　O God, how many times have I pleaded my case to leave
　　　　　　this invented destroyer
　　　　　　that seeks escape from the child in me, that seeks to
　　　　　　　　indulge the child
in me
　　　　　in every whim so that it never stops eating candy
　　　　　so that it cannot smell
　　　　　or see its own destruction.
Every drunken night
every time I drugged myself beyond recognition
every time I spoke words that lime-dust-powdered the heart
every time I bullshitted and ranted and raved my adventurous verve
　　　　　was the dark iron bridge opening and closing
　　　　　its mouth—
I sat in the boxcar and saw the whole city unfold before me—
tall spires of square buildings with clips of lit windows
　　　　　deep-set squares in the night
　　　　　and then the unsuspecting bridge opened and I was
　　　　　　laid open
　　　　　to where I should be
not the city, but the dark starry universe, the starlight of Me,
　　　　　not scuttling in fear through narrow aisles

hustling for drugs and flesh
        where people were selling bloody chunks of meat
        ringing chickens' necks
        screaming at one another before shelves of severed
            pigs' heads,
        violating their integrity
as I have done all my out-of-control life.
        God, had I a single prayer on my lips
        I would plead on my knees
        to help me get by this bridge
        to take this bridge and dismantle it bolt by bolt
        but it is me!
            The face I invented to cover mine
            I am afraid of distance and space
            and the bridge ties two continents together
            who I am and where I've fled to
this dark ugly oppressive bridge
I have used to get me past my own hell, away from my own fears,
away from the child in me screeching for help and nourishment
        The BRIDGE
        darkens with my blood and is dark with so many
            wasted nights.

And this poem, brother, is an attempt
to wrench the time-frozen bolts loose
        I no longer belong beneath the city lights at night
        nor do I dream my place in one of those high-rise condos
        in an apartment with whiskey, women, drugs
        and music—
an attempt of words to crack the iron
and splay the cable braids
and in one great havoc
        of iron cracks and splinters
        take down go down be down bridge!
shaking the earth
and myself into
        the child again

into an unabridged self
feeling of wounds
and fear
and hate
and struggling around me.

For so long
I want to walk with you, son, in me
you the boy walked the narrow border of the bridge
and looked down on the waters of my own soul
roiling and rampaging with my discontent
and how you, son, climbed the cables
       looking for the inventor of this atrocity
       to call him back so you might have a hand
       in climbing down
       from a place you never intended to stay
and had you jumped, I would be dead;
the bridge would have collapsed
and been maintained
       by another man like me
       afraid to face his face in the mirror
       dreaming that his song lay in another place in the city
       rather than his own heart and soul and with his own tongue
       unabbreviated by booze or whiskey or drugs . . .

       Of things I have created simply to negate myself!
       I have ignored my friends' love
       my love for myself
       my own residence on earth
           because of this evil bridge
       created to flee from hordes of human beings suffering
       to deny it is so
       to blind myself from the hungry and loving and
           seeking and singing
and find
a way to flee from it all by constructing a bridge
that sets to see only city lights

to create a mirage that the world is only city lights at night
and in a shroud of darkness behind doors I can transgress every
      single human dignity
          and be vile, corrupt, slavering and drooling with greed
          and lust
and when the steel eyelids of the bridge open
I see a glimpse of the true stars
of my fragile place in the universe, of my beginning and my
      face . . .
          But a long time ago I created
          a man who would drink as well as any other—
          created a myth of a druggie
              to fit the fast crowd
              to be accepted
and therein went the first bolts of the bridge
covering the holes of wounds I could not heal myself with
      forgiveness or wisdom
and when the world receded from me
          I pounded in the creation
          of this bridge that became only a necessity
          for the moment, but then became me, my world, my
              need, my addiction
          my cover
from myself
and of myself
          and when a woman kissed me
          she kissed the black iron beams running under my
              cheeks and chin and lips
          when she held my hand
          she held the taut cables knotted with bolts
and it was the bridge that could hold the whole world's crossing
that could bear up under weight and wreckage and disappointment
bridge of bones and soul and life that became me to this day . . .

There is such a sadness to this bridge I have invented . . .
          Alone at times after a day of drinking with friends

driving home, I cross this bridge
thinking my life would be better
if I jumped off, or drove off,
    because when the sun sets and people who have struggled
hard for something in this life and love each other
    gaze at me passing, still the gypsy
    drunk and addict
    alone, crossing his bridge toward home
I sense this terrible tragedy about my life
and the boy in me
who wants this bridge destroyed
    and will hang
himself on the cables someday
    if I don't snip them—
I do not look on from the height of this bridge
nostalgically,
too many people have tossed themselves off—
nor do I romantically believe any lore as I look on the distant
    shorelined city's
    blaze of lights
    that I would like to have it all, money and love
none of this is true anymore.
    I want the bridge down
    to be taken and ripped away
    in one torrential killer-rage Niagara
        song-fall
        of who I really am
        on this earth . . .
I am not some drunken despot
arm-wrestling knife-pulling
gouging and growling beast
    I am a sweet child permeated with minty
        summer-morning resins
    rainfall leaves on the air
    I am a sweet loving child who abhors violence and is
        terrified of drugs

a child who loves embraces and kisses
more than swollen kisses and cursed words
          condemnations . . .
          bare-chested little boy playing under a roof drain
          splashing his legs and hands
          and laughing . . .
I am not his haughty bridge
that spans opposing contradictions of two evils
that connects two infected islands.
          It is a bridge
          built on fear
          to let the boy swim back and place his feet onshore again,
          a bridge
          that will not let the boy's difference
          be,
a bridge
of black rage that turns itself tighter
into itself
to hold itself together.
          A bridge in my rib cage,
          this terrible brooding bridge
          gives me exit
          and avenue
          to flee from the boy in me
          who was so hurt and abused
          and was afraid to rage and rage
and built in his small place
the first cable
he held to,
then the second cable
until the whole bridge was built
and offered him solace
          he didn't have to touch his tears roaring beneath him
          he didn't have to stay in one place
          he could run and run until he saw no hideous face
          that offended him.

The child made his bridge
out of desperation
and every time he looked back, he knew he left the tender part of
    himself behind,
he knew that he would have stayed and felt the wound
        but thirty-seven years later
        the bridge gapes open, a huge prehistoric carnivorous
        demon
and in the mauling lust of its snarl
        sees his sweet child face
        imbedded in the bridge's bowels . . .
        as the bridge slowly strangles him and the boy
        between two places
        in the middle
        the curse of having not been strong enough
        to choose
        to become
        to be
        to let go
        to give in
        to cry
        to
        live . . .

and let the small boy walk on the ground again
no height, no span, no forced observation point
where nothing can harm him
        stand
        and breathe
        and let the hurt
        and pain
        unravel
        as the bridge collapses
        letting go of both places the small boy never wanted
        neither the invention of freedom nor fugitive
        just his small hands

and feet working out a life for himself
on earth.
It was the dream last night
that spoke to the
            boy
            the bridge
            the bloody chickens, the chunks of hanging meat
            the crowds, the women, the fanfare
            the hubbub
            the pure hell the boy eyed and wept at
            and raged against
            that makes this poem
            real.

Fifteen

What kind of poem is appropriate?
I remember when we were fifteen and sixteen
raising hell at VIPs
            just before cruising you'd slick your hair back,
            throw some nice creased jeans on
            and a bright shirt,
you loved contrasting colors and excitement
and working at the Desert Hills Motel
you met Evel Knievel
and wouldn't stop talking about how one day
you were going to be rich, buy those silver
flame-resistant pants and jacket and shoot off like a rocket
in front of a Las Vegas crowd.

            Mostly, though, I remember we walked the dark streets,
            sharing our dreams, thinking aloud
            whether we'd be rich or happy,
                        live in the city or on a ranch,

and somehow we'd end up in a friend's room
listening to oldies but goodies,
laughing and combing our hair in the mirror
even though we had nowhere to go.

     I'd defend you in a fight,
     cracking jokes as we ran from cops,
     you'd rescue me from bullies jumping me,
     pulling up to a stop sign, I'd leap in the back window
          and you'd screech off burning tires.

Sometimes that Little Dipper in the sky
would tilt our way and all the luck in the world would pour
       down on us,
you'd snag a fine-looking chick,
     I'd hot-wire a car,
     we'd ride low, grinning like monkeys down Central,
     and I'd bust open a cigarette machine
          and we'd party on a hundred dollars in quarters,
          munching down burgers,
          and for you, always an ice-cold beer to wash it down.

We did it all, escaping from the orphanage,
basketball and marbles under the big outdoor shed,
you being the baddest hoopster, the sharpest shooter,
but always a quiet side to you
     from the wounds that never healed,
     from the dreams shattered in the dark all alone,
     from never getting the breaks you so much deserved,
and I ask myself
     what kind of poem can express the sweetness,
     the kindness, the pain and hurt
that swelled in you like a volcano, simmering red smoke
     from your always-hurting always-dreaming hurt?
What kind of poem,
now as I sit here late at night
with nothing but love for you, brother,

can I write
        to say you meant the world to me,
to holler and scream it's not fair?
All I can promise you is that in every ounce of dignity I have,
with every thought and feeling I experience
as I try to change this world from being so violent
        to a more peaceful place,
                all I can promise is that you'll be with me,
                        with the sweetness and patience and humor
                        and conviction you had,
there won't be a step I climb,
a night's sleep,
a morning I awake,
        that I won't smile in my heart
                for having a loving brother
                who just couldn't ever say it,
                        but who I knew had nothing but love
                                and more love in him.

You were cooler than Motown blues,
        styled sweeter than a Santana song,
        but sentimental fools we both were,
        you falling in love with every chick
                        who fluttered a dove-smile your way,
                        once you even made me drive all the way back
                        from Las Cruces
                        because you were heartbroken,
                        and my car broke down halfway
                        and I had to hitchhike under the desert sun
                        just to embrace you and be with you.

For a brother there is no better,
a friend no finer,
a companion to travel the journey with,
        honored, loved,
                rocking and popping
                all day long, my brother.

But your dying
made a rush of silver knives
explode through my soul,
cutting every tendon that controls my body
and in a huge surge of volcanic emotion
I want to fall on the ground and scream
at the injustice—

my heart completely shatters its composure
a fierce rumbling of pain drives a stake
from the center of my heart outward
and every flower bleeds tears at dawn,
leaves droop with green sadness,
the sand howls up in dust devils
dancing its death step
    and I want to stop the world from spinning,
    freeze the earth's axis with my cold grip
    and cry your life back,
    change the way your life had been,
    place my hands in your soul
        like a potter at the wheel
        and make a beautiful vase of your soul
        and fill it with fruit and flowers and candies
        and armfuls of brimming-over love—

at the hour of your death
I crush the clock fate carries,
and a sadness walks in me like rain
across the desert,
    carving gullies of grief,
    cutting the land with deep gouges
    where in the bottom I live
        never seeing sunrise again
          never seeing
          top-land life,
in the gullet of this grief I roam

like a mad elk seeking exit,
and finding none,
    only more curves, more turns,
    caught in the maddening maze of why you had to die
        now, why,
            why my lovely brother,
and then my angry tears splash and spill over me
and in the reflection I see what a sweet brother you were,
what a lovely soul you had
as a child running around Grandma's house,
I remember your bright smile, your inquisitive eyes,
your adventurous heart,
how you dreamed for and prayed
to find a place in life where you could feel comfortable,
where you could prosper
    because you had so much love and sweetness
    to share with the world,
    always my hero, Mieyo, always my companion in the dark,
excited dreamer, catching the sun in your hands,
you played with it all day as if it were your close friend.
In the morning
your bright brown eyes, your sad life, your sweet heart
so filled with compassion and enthusiasm for dreaming.

And in the final dream
in dorm three, as a barn boy you rose
before dark and headed to the barn
to milk the cows, feed the pigs,
and while the rest of us were in church
you were eating just-baked donuts at the bakery,
trading marbles brimming a knee-high milk can
for La Parrot pomade or a new shirt,
    favorite of the nuns,
    slender, Elvis sidelong glance
        and polished suede shoes
        with your ducktailed black hair

slicked back, you grinned
into the camera standing before
        our *Virgen de Guadalupe* grotto,
you grinned into the camera lens
as if you knew the world
was awaiting your arrival,
out there beyond the orphanage fences
the world laid out the white linen,
butlers, servants, maids hustled
back and forth in black and white uniforms,
        and for a while you forgot
                Father and Mother had abandoned you,
                you forgot
                how the cruel and brutal world could be,
                all dressed up
                making your First Communion,
                and words came easily to you,
                your heart was pleased that you were going to be rich,
                famous, singing as the third person in the Everly Brothers,
                swaying like a windblown kite
                        gently in the clouds, all alone in the blue
                                        dream.

So how do I explain your horrible death?
I turn up the radio loud so I don't have to think,
but the day and scene come to me,
wearing your turquoise buckle,
Polo shirt, Wrangler jeans, Nike tennis shoes,
a black money-pouch belt,
you were riding your bicycle down that alley
in West Palm Beach
with a wad of money on you
when someone came at you from behind
and hit you with a bat/pipe
for an instant you went into a coma,
a fleeting second when you breathed with relief
that it was over,

and then you died
in an alley,
robbed, pockets turned out, bleeding
under the sun, face at peace,
body rigid,
    the flame of your spirit
      sparking as it ricocheted against pebbles,
      dazed, suddenly
like a fledgling sparrow fallen out of its nest,
your wings hurriedly flapped, beating the air
until the lightness of being
hummed through you,
    and you inhaled your new breath, young again,
    eternal again, at peace again.

*   *   *

You worked the system, Mieyo,
like a yo-yo or top,
you had the master keys to the Coke room,
to the wine cupboard in the priest's quarters,
even as an adult in court
    with twenty DWIs
    you never did time,
    the judge somehow let you go,
    and standing on the sidewalk outside the jail
    you'd give that sweet childish grin,
again you'd worked the system—
as if it were nothing more than a playground
with teeter-totter and monkey bars and merry-go-round
you still the skinny knock-kneed kid
with brown suspicious eyes
    still dreaming that one day your dreams would all materialize
    like a hammer, a carpenter's leather bag
    smelling the fresh-milled pine boards
      as you got out of your pickup
      climbed up on the deck of another house

you were building,
banging all day, yelling at crew guys
to hammer, get it down,
so you could split and drink a nice cold beer.

*　*　*

Whose fault was it?
Who or what stands guilty of your death?
Now, as my daughters outgrow their beds,
strong and big as horses roaming fields at dawn,
up at the West Mesa where other murdered bodies have been found,
we parked on the rim and overlooking the city
of Albuquerque
we prayed and cried for you,
cried that you never had the time to visit,
that you spent most of your life in pain
and doused the burning with booze,
injected the wounds with whiskey, beer and wine,
numbed them with drugs,
shared your lonely nights with crack whores
and liked them,
who while pregnant and dilated
on the verge of having a baby
roam the alleys smoking crack,
shooting up meth,
snorting cocaine,
inside you too, Mieyo,
was a maimed child whipped with hangers by uncles,
raped as a child by two suited gringo fags,
abandoned by alcoholic parents,
each day you took out your knife
and carved your name in bark
on a dream-tree,
because one day you believed what you desired and fevered
for would meet you like a lover
under the tree

and you'd be happy,
          just like in the fairy tales.
But from that dream-tree the leaves went gray and blew away,
lightning struck it and blackened the boughs,
the ground was poisoned by bloodletting in fights,
          on mornings when you woke up with swollen eyes,
          broken ribs, bruised and cut
          from getting beat up again,
          and that dream-tree petrified, cracked in winter like
               ice
          and stood out in the landscape, a jagged reminder
               of a broken dream,
               a thorn piercing your heart,
          an arrow you could never pull out,
          every day stabbing you again, again and again . . .

                    *   *   *

And how simple life could have been!
You never asked for much space in the world,
just a small room,
always overly clean, everything had to have a place,
except you never found yours in the world,
the light kept burning but you never reached it,
mostly darkness, mostly groping,
mostly stumbling,
               but you kept rising every day,
insisting in your heart that love and peace had to be
out there somewhere,
and you went looking for it in bars,
alleys, motel rooms, dealers' evil dens,
your soul a gold-toothed pirate laughing at fate,
always testing the waters and going beyond into the darkness
to the end of the world
to discover a new land where you could hang
that big white cowboy hat and take off your boots
     and rest a bit
          sipping that coffee you loved to drink each morning.

* * *

But I'm hurting, brother, for you,
I'm hurting so bad for you,
        someone has taken a sword and ripped my soul in half
        as if it were a mere white paper
        and even if I know I got angels
        guarding me, a whole army of angels
                guiding me through the dangerous wastelands,
                I'm telling you, Mieyo, I won't go down,
        your death won't be meaningless,
        I'm promising you that I don't understand
        how my father, mother and you all died violent deaths
        and I won't let it rest
                but I'll sing in the fields, roads, on stages
                at every community center and college
        and transform your hurt, my hurt, their hurt
        into that dream of peace you believed in
        I promise I'll open my heart
        and come with twice as much power and love and
                understanding
        as those thugs who use guns and drugs to control people,
        for every one that they addict
        or hurt or maim,
        I have five set free, loving, growing, embracing
        empowered
people who will join me in this dream of yours
        to make a more peaceful world. I will!

* * *

I hear your voice
coming up from the casket
whispering that all is well, soft as the white silk
cushioning the coffin sides,
more comfortable than the red cotton pillow
your voice rises
from that square box, your face placid,
serenely still, your body from working thirty years

outdoors building houses finally
relaxes, your pose like a tall pine tree
poised alongside a cliff, bearing itself to the sky and wind with
      dignity,
offering refuge for birds and attracting the passing eye
to wonder on life, on time, on the passing
of love and the richness of memories.
Your voice was always vulnerable,
those desert blosssoms that risk appearance
at spring then at night
are sniffed and eaten by insects, toads, coyotes,
shivering a moment in their pristine elegance
beneath a black mesa moon,
stationary above a village with chimney smoke
spiraling up toward the Dipper
where their piñon smoke collects and converges
with the endless universe.

I want to talk with you,
induce your spirit to guide and bless me,
and I'll pray each morning for your spirit,
light my incense, glance at the flickering
candle on my altar before sleep,
think of you, pray for you, meet you
in a dream with our fishing poles,
tramping down through thick grass to a mountain river
balancing out on a fallen tree limb
over the water to look at trout
shimmering below in the shallows in mossy branches.

You loved nature,
always spoke about that cabin in the mountains
with a big fireplace, loved
solitude, loved cowboy coffee and prairie roads
where no one could touch you,
where all your failures in the past could blow

away in the dust storms
and where the IRS couldn't catch you
nor the car dealership insurance company
hounding you for late payments.
most of the week working, gut aching, back sagging,
bending over and carrying up and holding in
and sawing in half and edging and shimmying

you looked grubby and unkempt—
but when you dressed up, not a male model
in slick magazines looked more handsome
or inviting to females than you—
you shone, you were magnetic, you were innocent,
and your dream for a good life radiated
from your brown eyes, your dimpled smile,
your new shirt and new jeans, your polished cowboy boots
and big fancy rodeo buckle.

Beans, tortillas, eggs and red chile,
robust and muscled, vitamin-charged,
you loved sitting in a chair and watching the morning,
watching birds act when they're excited about spring,
when the climate abruptly changes and they start
chattering away like kids at a circus.

There was nothing in life you loved more
than not worrying
            just not worrying.

*   *   *

You always hung with workers,
unshaven, groggy-talking
rough-fisted, plough-horse-shouldered
                              guys
wrapped in tattered coats and torn jeans, scuffed
wallets conformed to work habits,

huffing warm breath on cold mornings,
intent on nailing, getting it done,
with no futures, no past, transient carpenters
trains left in the city
and who picked up papers the next morning
answering laborers' ads,
who stayed on because they learned how to put up walls,
build from the ground up
houses for others who were making it,
always others, always
        standing in their rock-hard work boots
        laced up, packing up tools and saws and levels,
        tape measures, cocked caps back
brows burned and prematurely wrinkled
souls stained with days
that spilled on their innocence like cheap purple wine
on an immaculate white tablecloth.
        It just never came out,
        no matter how hard they scrubbed.
        Never came out.

           *   *   *

Let this prayer
float like a white moth to your soul,
always striving toward the light, Mieyo,
dimly lit like a scuba diver's light underwater
as it goes farther and farther out to sea,
a prayer, sweet brother,
with all our voices calling out love for you,
we gathered here like a solitary guitar, each of our hearts
red guitar strings you strum upon in the silence
to make music sadly moving as we grieve your passing,
but you'll never leave our thoughts,
never be far away from our hearts,
every evening when I look at the stars,
when the sun rises, when wind blows gently
at the tips of grass and they slightly bend,

when gardens start to sprout small chile plants,
when crowds at basketball games rise and yowl excitedly,
when a father's laughter joins a child's first words,
when the hummingbird blends into the air
blurring by like a jeweled ruby
all of these will reflect off my bones like a mirror
of memories and I'll think of you
whom I love so much—
    but no one can undo fate,
        no one can reach into the heavens
            and crush the clock and turn it back
            so humbly, all of us pray,
            continually raising out hands to the sky
            working the hard work,
                with dignity,
            standing up for what we believe,
            being there, brother, being there
            to continue onward
            as you would have wished,
            loving each other,
                a strong *familia*, brother,
                strong men and women
                holding each other, loving each other,
                  caring for each other,
                    amen, brother, amen,
                    we go with you, you stay with
        us,
                  we are not parted, brother,
                  we just live in different forms,
                  you spirit and us flesh,
                  together
                  we travel, brother,
                    with love and dignity.

Sixteen

For the longest time
    I haven't been able to cry.
    Tears start to come while I'm watching a movie,
    tears start to come,
swelling my whole body, a tulip starting to open under moon
    then the petals of my eyelids
    stiffen
    and something in me braces
and I don't cry.
    When we crashed into a telephone pole
    my dad yelled at me not to cry,
    I was terrified, almost killed—
    but I didn't cry.
    I couldn't cry because men don't cry.
    When the dog bit me on the leg I couldn't cry,
    when Joey died I couldn't cry—
    how cool it would feel
    to have a tear slide down the corner of my eye
    on my cheek
    to the curve of my lip,
    where I could taste it—
    but I don't cry.
    Something blocks the paths, channels
    under my skin.
    Tear ducts are red cracked clay,
    for thirty years,
    drought-famined,
    since I was eight when I got a beating for crying.
    My heart an open furnace door,

rage seething for tears to cool it down,
but coal-shoveling men keep feeding it,
don't cry don't cry don't cry.
I want to untie my hands like a tired boxer's gloves
and lay them down on the table, gripped in their tight
clench of defense,
and I want to grow new hands,
open flowers
moistened by my tears.
I love the colors blue
and brown.
I'd love
to touch my chapped cheeks
and whisper in tears
my compassion.
But I've always had to stop it up in me, hold my breath back,
keep my mouth shut tight
so as not to cry.
Man, I cry,
and it's a lie I don't.
I embrace my brother and pray shoulder to shoulder.
I kneel and kiss earth,
and I cry—
if only I could cry.
Don't translate my tears into thought,
I want to sob autumn tears on my window,
streaking the pane, blurring the world.
I want to fill every hold in my heart with glimmering tear pools,
fill my kitchen sink with tears,
just thinking of me not crying all these years
makes me want to cry,
but I been taught not to cry—
big people don't cry, people say,
ain't those alligator tears, boy,
can't fool me with those tears—
bullshit!
Fooling no one but myself not crying—

step aside—
I'm going to cry
until my shirt is drenched
and my hands are shimmery wet
with tears
running down my face, on my arms,
my legs and breast
and you have to look at me
because I'm drowning your manly ways in my tears,
to get back my tears.
I'm crying until there isn't a single tear left,
crying
for what we been through not crying,
how we fooled ourselves thinking men don't cry.
I'm crying on the bus, in bed, at the dinner table, on the couch,
enough to float Noah's boat,
let out the robin of my heart,
bringing me back my own single shoot of greening
life again—
and you go fuck yourself
dry-eyed days,
here I come,
giving you a Chicano monsoon season,
here comes this Chicano crybaby,
flooding prison walls,
my children's bedrooms,
splashing and slinging tears
up to my ankles,
planting rice and corn and beans
in fields glimmering with my tears,
and all you dried skinned nut-cracking ball whackers,
don't want to get your killer bone-breaking boots wet,
step aside,
because I'm bringing you rain.
Good-byes were crying events—
good-bye to Grandma, to my brother,

friends, my neighborhood,
teachers and other boys,
and I never shed a tear,
    though I felt them coming up in me.
    I bit my teeth down hard to hold the tears back,
    lowered my face and thought about something else.
    I kept hearing voices in me
    telling me not to cry, don't cry, don't cry!
Boys don't cry,
leave yourself open,
become liable to get an ax in your heart by some noncrying fool,
be a sissy,
puto, you be hurting
yourself if you cry.
    I hurt when I didn't cry,
    all those times when I didn't cry,
    ashamed to in front of people,
    fearful others would think I'm not a man,
    fearful I'd be made fun of,
whole groups of us heard tragic news
and no one cried
because it ain't right—
    we need to weep—
    get up in the middle of the night
    and cry, like a woman's hips and stomach convulse during
    childbirth, we need to give birth
    to that terrible convulsion of tears,
    weep for those we never wept for,
    let the legs shake and arms embrace you
    in a junkie habit for tears,
weep for the poor in prison
taken from their families,
the field-worker's daughter
eaten by cancer from pesticides,
    and weep
    for all those homeless

who couldn't meet mortgage payments,
those sleeping under bridges,
and the hopeless,
cry our differences into a lake
where we can all cleanse our good-byes and apathy,
papas cry for their children,
let children cry in my arms,
men cry in my arms,
women cry in my arms,
let us all cry
after lovemaking and fighting,
make crying a prayer,
a language made of whimpers and sniffles and sobs,
cry out loud, louder, crybaby, cry! Cry! Cry!

Seventeen

Someone placed a piece of wheat bread on the top of a
    cinder-block wall.
I suppose for birds.
I took it as a subversive act against the yelling and killing in
    the world.
In the piece of bread was hope.
What I thought had been lost came back, the kind act,
    needing no audience clapping or
award, the silent act of generosity and thoughtfulness
brought back the endangered species, the kind act.
Anonymous yet encompassing all of humanity.
Faceless yet bearing all our faces.
Dipping into our lonely world as a child's hand in the font,
    in the cool holy water.
The black stinkbug and furry bumblebee sensed the
    fragrance on the air.
Peach mush on the sidewalk gloated golden scribbles,

bleeding vaginal juice into sullen seeds that crack the
        concrete in celebration
of bread left for birds.
I learned again what I usually forget—
to start my day with a prayer, prayers in so many guises,
some on cinder-block walls, some in work boots under beds,
others in a smile, a hello, a tear,
    the crane on the lake that had vanished for months, until
        one day when the old woman for
the hundredth time visited the shore, saw it again sitting on the
    old salty pole, how its return lifted
from her soul the fog and allowed the dawn to radiate in a
    blinding sunstorm over the water of her
soul,
        a white feathered prayer.
    I heard the news this morning that my cousin Rose is going
        to prison for a long time.
    Place bread on the window ledge of every jail cell.
    My stepsister was in the same cell with Rose, and they both
        huddled in a blanket in the
holding cell.
        My stepsister gave Rose the tennis shoes on her feet before
            leaving and walked out of jail
barefooted.
        Indian Market is happening in Santa Fe
        as it does every year in August. Three thousand Indians
            pandering paintings, smiling their
pot-smiles,
        dancing and grunting and ahooing for the White Man's
            green wampum.
        Chicanos and Chicanas are Indios, still at war with
            the enemy who would
ignore starving children, neglect the elders,
        from the tip of Chile to Anchorage, Alaska,
        La Raza are being jailed for speaking out against oppression,
        executed in Chiapas for writing about slaughters,
        and here in my own hometown my cousin was just given

fifty years' hard time,
my stepsister beat up and raped by rednecks,
and I praise the hand that set out the bread on the wall for
        the birds,
I let my dogs in and they curl down by the couch
I peek into my other daughter's bedroom and she snores
        deeply, in a dream that offers reprieve from the
madness
        of slavery my people endure where they are paid a dollar a
        day and die from pesticide
poisoning.
        The pueblos with their gambling casinos turn their faces
        from Chicanos,
        they treat us as they were treated by the White Man,
        Hang Around the Fort and Trading Post Indians who have
        forgotten to give bread to the birds.
        In prison we defended the Indians, we backed their play,
        they were us we were them,
        we were hands they were hands, we were bread they were bread,
        we were eagles they were eagles—
        at the plaza they resemble yellow parakeets in cages,
        twittering away on a swing, singing for the tourists who fill
        their feeders with coins.
        The coins are not to buy bread.

        The supple-tongued reasons for betrayal
        are never as real as reasons for freindship.
                                Driving the other day,
        I saw a small brown girl and boy tugging on a tree branch.
        I knew that in their play
        resided the answers to peace, that their imaginations made
        the tree branch
and the shade and looming tree a kingdom for people to live in
        peace,
to love one another, to laugh and love and share.

Eighteen

    After summer-evening rain in August, dormant memories stir up. Kids defy gravity on BMX bicycles, sailing easily over self-made mud ramps and slip-'n'-slide, skid and scoot, tires cleat dirt track. Black crows line the wooden fence like lascivious tenants ogling the landlord's gorgeous daughter undressing in the window, watching, tsk-tsking the handmade world of youth. The heirs of fortune—ants seize upon grass seeds carrying the grain jewels past graffitied walls painted over with blocks of white, carrying seeds over mounds of mown grass moldering to yellow mulch behind backyard fences.

    The air is moist and heavy with stable dung.

    There are no old houses in the suburbs.

    In the suburbs, Fridays have replaced dreams.

    But children save the suburbs, their souls and hearts are
        raucous barns with squawking hens and mooing cows
        and whinnying colts. Their smiles and laughter
        fresh as hand-squeezed bubbly pailed milk.

    Prairie doves skim the wet arroyo.

    It stops raining.

    A love story begins.

    The earth disrobes and embraces the rain, her flesh swells
        and reels with the rain in blood-red lips of lovemaking.

    The earth and rain are two peasant rebels who haven't seen
        each other in months—in blossoms, trees, hedges,
        earth and rain twist and knot and twine and weave a
        magic.

    Garden rakes and shovels lean against walls like murderers
        lounging against the feed store wall watching from
        under bristling hat brims

and wheelbarrows slouch on haunches gloomily gazing on
the lovers like churchgoing thieves on the church
collection box.
Lewd gutters spread rainy rumors, babbling to the prairie
doves that elegantly search the wetland of our hearts
for entry into heaven's house.
The red clouds on the horizon unscroll like marble pillars
crushed by a thousand stampeding stallions and raging
mares, trampling across the skies in furious dream-
making gallops that remind us suburbanites of our
dreams we one day sighed and in our exhale released
our yearnings for who we dreamed we might be and
things we might achieve in life.
Our flesh hangs on our bones like old military uniforms
waiting for the war that would make us generals and
saviors and heroes.
Our lips need more movement, our tongues more than the
taste of food, our teeth more than meat, our hands
more than steering wheels and jewels and papers . . .
our sensibilities yearn for the ephemeral seed to crack
in our faith and we blow the husk and chaff from our
palms and witness the seed of compassion and dream
root in our palm skin, break blood in the blade of seed
need, rooting its tendril roots in our bone marrow.
What if we had plants growing from our flesh as the
earth from her soil? What if we had names given us
from hearts shattered like meteorites colliding with
planets, from intergalactic travel, from knowing other
languages, from accepting others, from loving strong
and hard, from forgiveness and strength,
we would have our true names.
Art gives us new names, names our hearts apple tree, peach
or grapevine, oven bread, sugar . . .
our key-hole lives deprive us of so much,
but each dawn gives us reason for raging at the door and
shattering it, indulging in what we love before the
light on the horizon finally vanishes.

When I went out this morning to jog along the arroyo, the
    sun and the light and the green blades of river reeds
    glowed with the masculine pride of a godparent,
and for someone like myself, who had no baptism, whose
    mother worked in a whorehouse and father stumbled
    in gutters drinking drops of stale wine and whiskey
    from discarded bottles in alleys,
I praise the morning's beauty,
praise the Little Leaguer kids playing baseball at the park,
    the ponytailed coach (a Dead fan) underhands the ball
    and a skinny, grime-necked kid swats the ball and all
    the munchkins move like minnows in a current toward
    the ball,
praise the ant crushed under the jogger's Nike
the frog squished under the truck's tire,
the Rollerblading parent dashing around the park pushing
    his infant's carriage ahead of him,
the fiftyish man pruning and mowing the lawn, wearing his
    college T-shirt and shorts, snipping the glossy leaves
    from the walkway,
praise the weeping willow tree that grew far over the wall
    and shades the sidewalk pedestrians walk on,
praise the ten-year-old kid with his new helmet and new
    bike, perched on his seat waiting for traffic to pass,
the yard-salers on Saturday morning,
the mean truckloads of jowled Indians refusing to let
    motorists in, grumpy from too many greasy breakfasts,
praise the Chicano selling cocaine, the woman who lets
    mountains of laundry mold on the floor for years, the
    junk man who spends a life towing and tinkering with
    dead-hulk iron and steel,
praise those who never get anything done,
who are put on earth to make others miserable,
praise our problems and shortcomings and faults,
praise those who make appointments and are always late
    and those who never show,

praise those who get drunk, get high, who don't care if they
     die or live, who do business on a handshake,
because without them, the morning sun would not look as
     beautiful,
nor would your garden be so splendid, each blossom and
     petal raising itself like a country peasant liberated
     from oppressive tyrants,
hordes of cheering flowers raising their arms to sing their
     freedom and carpet hot concrete and brick with soft
     petals,
blistered and drying pale rose hearts,
blossoms trampled by misery that rules the wasteland,
blossoms urging us to follow the path.
I turn on an old record by Elvis singing about falling in love
and sip my hot coffee and wonder of the names I've had
     and creatures
I've been in this life.

Nineteen

I needed the break
     a hard-edged bone jag stick-break
     plunged into the heel
     gnawing it,
          until consciousness
          rises to the surface
               without suffering
               without pain
               with what was needed—
for me
it was going to Creede, Colorado,
     with my two girls and Cindy
bunking up at the Blue Creek cabin
then taking the old mining trail

           up East Willow Road
           up the mountain.
We could see its snowy summit
        as we cut in and out of pines
           on ribbed gravel
the raging Rio Grande
           moiling, cloud-bursting
               fast-moving current
               on the side of the dirt road
               we wowing
                   at trees growing out of rocks
                   riding alongside
sheer-cut mountains,
in toward narrow canyons,
until we came to a round-off
           clearing of dirt where the gravel smoothed
           into a circle for highway department crews and trucks
           cutting and clearing forest roads;
           went left and the craggy, boulder-studded
           fallen logs
           clawed the upland winding trail
               and we decide to cross the gushing creek
               Cindy and I out
               climbing the mountain
               lifting wind-wrenched fallen aspens off
                   the trail.
It was an amazingly, beautifully impassable trail,
the kind of trail one takes
when he doesn't want to see people anymore.
           Chamisal, Marisol and Branden
               in the Isuzu jeep
               Marisol weaving in and out slowly over
sharp granite, massive stones
               scudding the oil pan
               rocking the jeep back and forth,
                   nosing down steeply
                   jolted,

banged under rocks
            round Us
            rocks, rocks, rocks
            to keep anything without hoof or wing out
        but a poet and his daughters
        with Cindy, a visionary friend,
we kept climbing up and down, crossing another creek with
        rushing water
high at the door windows,
            but having fun, laughing, enchanted
            watching Marisol fishtail across mud-bog fields,
            splash-crash into roiling rapids
            coming out dripping
                under pine branches
                keeping the summit within sight,
we slammed, whacked, removed fallen logs,
inched over rocks, hit hard, bumped dirt,
            nosed up, scraped back end,
            creaked slowly,
                creeping our way over the last hill
                where we all stopped and stared
                in awe of the broad meadows below
                at the foot of the peak
                meandering with creeks
                a waterfall arching out from the rocks,
                    spilling out on ponds
                    beavers had built houses all around
                    and we were silent, infused with its green
companionable spirit.

In two days
we caught over a hundred brookies.
Their colors dazzle the eye,
mesmerize the heart
blue, red, orange, black spots
dark bodies with white and red spots
inside blue circles,

I found a placid pool
beyond the waterfall
and the second my worm hit the water
a trout snagged it, bucked, rearing
                              in its wild
born-from-waterfalls ways,
        never imagining such a thing
as a hook,
        fighting against my reeling in,
my rod bent to splintering
then tugging, reeling in
and drawing it up to the shore,
hoisting it on the grass
where it never dreamed of needle-nose pliers in its throat
gripping the hook,
taking it out as I crouched and watched it gasping,
eyes bubbling out, turning to rubbery gel
until I slipped it on my rope
        with other captives
        still flailing,
                flapping against the crude barbaric power
        the waterfall never told it of,
                this two-legged menace
                who had just killed it
                ate it,
                        somewhere
                in the vast night sky
                        its fish spirit swallows
shimmering flecks of light
and whirls in comet-tail whooshes
under glinting whitewater starlight,
puckering dark hole mouths
waiting for my spirit to shimmer by
        where I'll flail and fight
        for my life as they have for theirs.

Twenty

The peregrine falcon has been taken off
the endangered-species list—
how many things come back if we prepare
their homecoming?
      We all have roads in us
      winding within our arteries
      into distant hills of memories
      roads going from the incident
when we realized our mothers were human
and our fathers seldom spoke their feelings
but were good men.
      What we don't find on the roads
we travel is our own redemption.
We see signs symbolizing our shortcomings,
we remember lovers who were entwined in limbs
dreaming in sunrise on a bed
when our dreams floated like dandelion fibers
on bright chill breezy mornings.
We've all turned up the radio on autumn mornings
driving under a golden canopy of cottonwood branches
with the leaves glimmering sunlight
and Stevie Wonder celebrated our happy moments.
But the road turns
and the drums pound our sacrifice of innocence
on the Rio Grande shores and we find ourselves dancing
on sheer strength, beckoning for a willingness
to return our hearts to again believe in life's wonder.
We learn in our quiet moments
our weaknesses, like lost summers

with a lover on a beach or in woods,
the intense passion we felt and the sparkling
of dew-dripping leaves on moist pine-needled ground
surrounding us, blessing us with sight
to see ourselves in a momentary stillness of pure humility and
     passion,
how we truly are to ourselves
     fragile and impeccably beautiful,
     restoring our hearts
     like afterlove-tousled bedsheets
we spread evenly and pat out,
     preparing it for the lovers again.
Like most, I've gotten lost,
wondered which road would take me to happiness
and choosing the wrong ones gave me permission
to change, go crazy, get stranded, encounter God.
     I sometimes see a Sanchez tour bus
     on I-25 going north, humble faces of tourists
staring out the tinted window as the guide
in a conductor's cap points out pueblos
by the Rio Grande—as the bus was going forty,
I'm the one who jumped out of the back door
never a humble viewer in a tourist group,
     guided by stars and a raging pulse to live,
to experience life by crossing lines
I never intended to cross,
where I found myself, prepared
a nest for the peregrine falcons in my own life
to return, trusting me again,
my heart came back, my soul
saw me standing alone in the desert,
saw me ridiculed and mocked,
saw that I didn't have the strength to do it on my own,
and returned
to give me love and faith,
and I did it
on a suspended driver's license.

Twenty-one

Pause to think of death
        how I am half death, half life
        how languid wild grass stalks taller than the fence
        how undulating hilled horizon   red sky   dark hills
        engraves on me my own mortality
        how my body is a piñon husk I spit on sandstone
            cliff-rock
        how my body is the rough-stick eagle nest encircled
            on an overhanging ledge where my feathered
                spirit perches
            from which I can see my whole mountainous
                lifetime.
Pause to think of death
        when I see windswept flowers in the ditch
        and think how I floated downstream too
        in flowered love with life.
We have always crossed borders, always been half this half that
Aztecas canoed from island to island
Spanish roughhoused rafts across the Rio Grande
my daughters inner-tube the same river now.

Pause to think of death
when I see the apple my daughter left on the table
        half gnawed
when I see berries half pecked by birds
when I hear in the cool black stone obsidian
        the crow's caw-caw-caw
        in the cackled cracks.

My life is a willowing weed in the ditch current,
bass strings on a cello unfurling,
soft clapping hands to the wind, caving in the sandy sides of my
    years
        I run between
        toward the silent gate awaiting my arrival,
          where the huge mastiff of my spirit, sopping wet, will
              slop water everywhere
          shaking life off
          and curl before a warm fire and snore.

*   *   *

I felt light the other day,
a surge of minuscule cracklings that comes
when you're clean—
out the window, an instant of bliss.
      It was the sad exhilaration that comes
when you embrace an old familiar friend
who's been gone for a long time.
      I was happy my body was again grinding out the spark
      to restore my spirits.
It was a day to remember, a penny I stuffed in the coin purse
of my heart to keep and hope and pray many more come—
      the adrenaline rush made me feel
if I had a tight rope stretched
      across two continents I'd walk it in a storm.
When I'm healthy and clean I feel
      God grubbing in my bones,
      digging a pit in my heart,
      filling it with dried cow manure, cottonwood bark
and cedar wood chips,
and after fires burn down, he fishes me out
with a stick,
      dark, black, brown-sprinkled horsehair
      that evaporates on touching me,
making feathery edges of my hands and feet

elegant and healing, prepared for flight.
　　　But I hadn't prayed for a few days, which I usually do,
　　　kneeling at my bed and asking for willingness
to be true to my heart.

Going to L.A. without praying,
I sat with Anska sipping a cognac, then another, and another,
then wine, a little tequila, more wine, grapefruit juice and vodka,
　　　discussing movie scripts,
　　　surprised to find she lived next to Ramon, a friend of mine;
　　　grog-headed and stomach-sick the next morning,
I needed to pray, I was cracked.

An Iranian limo driver picked me up from the Park Hyatt,
and on the way to the airport I felt so queasy
he found a café and we had breakfast,
lox and eggs and oatmeal, and while we ate, he explained how
　　　he'd come to America
five years ago, married a Salvadoran woman
and when he was describing his escape from Khomeini tyrants,
how he'd endured torture,
he spoke of the twilight, a time of day
when it's bright/dark together.
That was me, bright/dark together. Bright with hope,
dark with regrets.

Last night was a full moon. Suspended over the Rio Grande,
I watched it over the treetops,
thinking about the bad experiences
of boozing and drugging in my past,
how each was a dark spot on the jaguar's pelt,
it marked my hide as I roamed the jungle like a jaguar.
I integrate my dark times, yawning at the moon,
I sniff the leaves of my poem pages for blood,
remembering how I once
dragged myself in every night wounded
and bleeding,

and now I step carefully, alert, in love with life!
This morning, taken out from the dawn light
intact, containing my feelings,
holding the darkness with the light in my body,
brimming with a bright/dark together.

Twenty-two

When questions about love
dizzy lovers with
if one is too old or too young
for the other,
 or when ex-spouses rage
 in the night and seethe at dawn,
 when one's life lies behind like a smoldering
 wrecked plane
 look to the humble lilac bush in the garden
 or the stray dog
 or the chirping of birds you hear
 from your bed when you're lying silently
 wondering about it all,
  the open windows let in a cool draft,
  it's midsummer,
you're planning to leave, to change again,
to move to another city,
have faith that the lilac bush will bloom again,
that the years ahead have been hard-earned,
you deserve to smile and laugh and have that moment
when life stands still in the glass globe
you shook as a child during Christmas
  believing truly that
  there was a Santa Claus.
It may sound dumb,

but it's better than the savage behavior I've seen
      when ex-spouses
      act like they were never children or never dreamed of love.

Twenty-three

From wrought-iron trellises, petals wrinkle and bronze. There is an
oldness, an ancient remembrance that simmers from the dying
      season—the South
Valley is a clay urn, and all our hearts, like red oak leaves
      knee-high on the
ground along the Rio Grande bosque, all smolder blessedly up
      to the vast sky.
      Last night I selected a piece of ground to build a storehouse on.
With rake and shovel, I broke clods up, smoothed, tossed dirt in
      dips, smoothed,
raked, eyed the rectangle plot from a distance, raked and
      smoothed more.
      I thought of the peacefulness. Sky was hot iron in a furnace,
            blasted
in the sand-lined horizon, the sky became a holy blue bowl fired
      in the furnace
to a red-bronze, the color I am.
      In the darkening nightscape, I saw myself from a distance.
            White-
shirted figure leaned over a rake, lost in puffs of dirt sprayed up
      and wide
as he threw shovelfuls through the air.
      I was connected to my ancestors. They had left behind the
            earth
for me to work and praise. This small plot I raked at evening,
      smoothing and
leveling, they had left me. Like others are given, from generation to

generation, books, photos, wealth, pendants and diamonds
        handed down from
grandfather to grandchild.
        I am related to those of the earth, a parchment made of dust
I added my name to in this work. From a long line of warring
        and peaceful
people, my turn has come to lift a handful of dirt and fling it to
        the air,
as I would my soul—I would fling a part of me to the air
in praise of my life.
        The same to-and-fro motion of the arms,
        the same sweat glistening the brow,
        the same aches in the constantly bending back,
        the same crushing of clods and smoothing
        of the fine soft dark dirt,
        the same dust in the nostrils and dry throat
        they did and experienced thousands of years ago.
        And as the evening darkened, I stepped back and appraised
                my work—
        the shifting of dirt, breaking it down to my wishes:
        I wished a future for my daughters, a place to play and
                praise their living.
        I felt calm and fulfilled as I put away the shovel and rake,
        wearily walked back to the house
        for a cup of coffee, a plate of chili, beans and tortilla.
        Right above my house is flight path for Kirtland
                Air Force Base.
        I feel the same toward those gray-green dark war fighters
        roaring deafening in the sky in arrowhead formations,
        as did my ancestors when they saw the conquistadores on
                horses
        breathing deep and foaming at the mouth, stamping and
                snorting,
        the clamor of armor clanking in the midst of rough voices
        hollering orders. After the jets have gone by, they leave a trail
        of smoky clouds behind as did the horses passing villages.
        I keep inside me the secrets of earth, my religion with her,

so that if all else is destroyed, my love for earth and her people
lives on. My raking and shoveling is part of my religion.
Outside, I look up. The white trails of the jets against dark sky
waver and disperse. Above the jets, far away in the night sky,
the Maker of All Things sees the jets like four black flies
buzzing around the air. He from above and Earth from below,
myself in the middle, together we fight the pestilence
of these inhuman machines circling over corpses.

Twenty-four

Beauty when I walk sleepily downstairs to the kitchen
for a cup of coffee,
beauty when I kiss my oldest daughter off to school,
beauty when I wake not in a hungover stupor,
beauty when old friends call to tell me
they've been thinking of me,
beauty when I go back to my old village
where I remember myself an innocent child
and realize I still am,
beauty when the day's ashes burn low and are blown away
by proud stars, and I go bed early
feeling like a prisoner close to completing his time,
beauty when I lose my temper and feel awful
but the following day I'm much better,
as if the arthritic fingers of the flamenco guitarist
have limbered up and strum viciously at the strings
to cull forth his heart's murmuring blaze of life,
stoking the strings like an old man poking at embers
and blowing to get the fire going on a really cold day,
beauty when I waken my youngest daughter from her dream
and she kisses me,
beauty for the small things I have

this morning,
this moment, this world, which
doesn't depend on money, how new my car is,
if the stock market's gone up, how many slick deals
I've made or if the check's arrived,
beauty depends on remembering who we are.

Twenty-five

There is a light in us,
a spirit that foams forth into the world
with our most powerful aspects
like a swollen ripe apple,
its tight skin gleaming a soft phosphorescence
on the blue air bulging with light,
     the apple like a medieval friar
     bursting with energy
     to toll those taste buds
          like bells in the tower,
          groaning with masculine happiness,
          the rough joys of plucking apples from the orchard
          and biting into one
               with the feverish relish of a jaguar
               licking water from a forest pond
                    after a night kill.
The apple's blood rings my lips
stains my fingers—
the tree
all alone in the middle of the field
          spreads its branches of light
          radiant
          without prayer or forgiveness.
               *   *   *

A praising morning,
when my hands become gifted
brown pigeons and everything I touch becomes a window ledge
in the sun,
        when my hands exalt the dry climate of the prairie
        and trust in God again,
        bending to touch a small blue flower
        my hands in pious, prayer gesture,
                believe flowers have spirits
                whose petals are genuine signs of gratitude
                                for breathing color.
It's praising morning,
        when I praise my old sneakers that have carried me
        down many a ditch bank and running path by the river,
        my hands, clenched appendages of piety,
        surrender like virginal maidens to the world's textures,
                wolf puppies sniffing at the sunrise,
                absorbed by every pebble and grain of dust
                I spin in,
                connecting opposites, bringing four directions
                humbly into a blurring center,
a maddened butterfly spinning its cocoon in,
I remake myself,
like a composer's hands connecting all the music
from all the musicians in the orchestra this morning,
into a fierce midair fluttering of my soul
                that curves itself out of me into air
                with passionate emphasis of the kettle drum:
                        Bam! Boom!
I want to know who you are.

                *   *   *

Begin this day entering the hours
that curve like glass bell jar,
                the sandy hours wind away like curving roads on air,
                disappearing, dipping and surfacing again

                straight
to the Ashram, soaking in Baba's love—

In my youth, I had fleeting insights into heaven
on mescal,
but my spirit hurt for words to speak, a speech
that would convey my being and express my experience.

Onward from the Ashram, past Chicanos
standing at the roadside with a shovel in hand, doing ditch work,
irrigating, watching the pleasant flow of water
        feed the seeds of their own primordial memories.

I leave Taos at noon, through the canyon's womb
to *El Santuario de Chimayo* in *Española*,
where the *padre* sprinkles me with holy water
and inside the small cool adobe interior,
        I kneel devoutly before *retablos de La Virgen de Guadalupe*,
bowing piously to *El Santo Niño de Atocha*,
        give my respects to Jesus' sacred heart of thorns,
and I think
        of all the Chicanos and Chicanas
                who've died from bullets, drugs or alcohol,
                whose obsidian eyes stare at me from photos
                        in handmade picture frames,
        commanding me to write poems on what their lives' visions
                were,
telling me with their silent brown eyes
                to live what I speak, to weave their young lives' truth
                into thick-braided vines we can use as footbridges,
                so that Uppidees and Downidees
                        can cross their individual worlds in a
                                way that frees them both
                        from fear—
                        sweep away the brittle bigotry piled at
                                the front door

like autumn leaves,
clean out those moldering mounds of
money
like rotten, decaying vegetables
and open yourself to let life come at you from four directions,
bills in the box, trash needs emptying, garden watering,
dogs need feeding, dishes washing,
be human, be real,
nourish that deep hungering desire
to be loved and love—

Twenty-six

For a woman—
we are yet to meet
yet your touch beats
like a drum over the air I breathe.

When the blood-filled dark wind
subsides
when the breathing knot of our lovemaking
is untied

I must leave.

And let not our words
draw widening rings of stone around us
circle black distance on everything
and leave us in the middle to stand alone.

Let our hearts awe the stone meanings of departure
like the Mayan ruins that record eternity,
our feelings loose grains from the great stone
that follow the wind.

Twenty-seven

Tire shop.
          I went down yesterday
to fix a leak in my tire. Off Bridge Street
there's a place, 95 cents
flats fixed,
smeary black paint on warped wood plank
between two bald tires.
I go in, an old black man
with a Jackie Gleason hat, greasy soft,
        with a mashed cigar stub in his mouth
and another old Chicano man
working the other
pneumatic hissing tire changer. The walls are black with rubber,
soot, blown black dust everywhere
and rows of worn tires on gnawed board racks for sale,
air hoses snaking and looped over the floor.
I greet the two old men,
        "Yeah, how's it going!"
No response.
They look up at me as if I just gave them a week to live.
        "I got a tire needs a tube."
Rudy, a young Chicano, emerges from the black part of the room
ponytailed and plump,
walks me out to my truck and looks at the tire.
"It'll cost you five bucks to take off and change."
        I nod.
He tells the old Chicano, who pulls the roller jack
        with a long steel handle outside,
and I wait in the middle of the grunting oval tire-
changing machines,

while the old guy goes out and returns with my tire.
        He looks at me like a disgruntled carny
        handling the Ferris wheel
for the millionth time
and I'm just another ache in the arm,
        a spoiled kid.
I watch the two old men work the tire machines,
        step on the foot levers that send the bars around,
flipping the tire from the rim,
and I wonder what brought these two old men to work here
        on this gray evening in February—
        are they ex-cons?
Drunks or addicts?
He whips the tube out. "*Rudy,*" he yells,
        and I see a gaping hole in the tube.
"Can't patch that," Rudy says,
        then in Spanish slang says, *"No podemos pachiarlo,"*
—we got a pile of old tubes over there, we'll do it for ten
dollars."
At first I think he might be taking me
        but I hedge away from that thought
        and I watch the machines work
the spleesh of air
the final begrudging phoof! of rubber popped loose
        then the holy clank of steel bar
against steel
and gently the old Chicano man, instead of throwing the bar
on the floor,
takes the iron bar and wipes it clean of rubber bits
        and oil
and slides it gently into his waist belt
        in such a way
I've seen a mother wipe her infant's mouth.
And I wonder where they live, these two old guys.

I turn and watch M*A*S*H on a TV suspended from the ceiling,
        six o'clock news comes on,

Huntington Beach blackened with oil.
Rudy comes behind me and says,
"Fucking shame they do that to our shores."
I suddenly realize how I love these workingmen
working in half dark with bald tires
like medieval hunchbacks in a dungeon.
They eat soup and scrape along in their lives—
how can they live, I wonder, on 95 cents a tire change
in today's world?
I am pleased to be with them
and feel how barrio Chicanos love this too—
how some give up nice jobs
in foreign places
to live by friends working in these places
and out of these men revolutions have started.

     The old Chicano is mumbling at me
     how cheap I am

when he learns my four tires are bald
     and spare flat,
     shaking his head as he works the tube into the tirewell.
I notice his heels are chewed to the nails,
his fingernails black,
his face a weary room-and-board stairwell
     of a downtown motel
given over to drunks and derelicts, his face hand-worn
     by drunks leaning their full weight on it,
wooden steps grooved by hard-soled men just out
     of prison, a face condemned by life to live out more days
     in futility.
I bid good-bye to the black man chomping his ancient cigar,
     the Chicano man with his head down
and I feel ashamed, somehow, that I cannot live
     their lives a while for them.
Grateful they are here, I respect such men who have stories
that will never be told, who bring back to me

my simple boyish days, when men
in oily pants and grubby hands talked in rough tones
        and worked at simple work, getting three meals a day
        on the table the hard way.

They live in an imperfect world,
unlike men with money who have places
to put their shame,
these men have none—
others put their shame on planes or Las Vegas trips,
these have no place
to put their shame on but their mothers
their kids
        themselves
unlike men who put their shame
on new cars
condos
bank accounts
so they never have to face their shame,
        these men in the tire shop
        have become more human with shame.

And I thought of the time my brother betrayed
        me leaving me at fourteen
when we vowed we'd always be together,
        he left to live with some rich folks
and I was taken to the detention center for kids
with no place to live—
        I became a juvenile
        filled with anger at my brother who left me alone.
These tire-shop men made choices
never to leave their brothers,
in them I saw shame with no place to go
        but in a man's face, hands, work and silence.
        And as I drove away, nearing my farm,
I saw a water sprinkler shooting an arc of water
        far over the fence and grass

it was intended to water—
      the fountain of water hitting a weedy stickered spot
that grew the only single flower anywhere around
        in the midst of rubble brush and stones
        the water hit
and touched a dormant seed that blossomed all itself
        into what it was
despite the surroundings.
And something made sense to me then
and I'm not quite sure what—
      an unconditional love of being and living,
      taking what comes one's way
      with dignity.
But that night in my dream
I cried for my brother as he was leaving,
      all the words I used against myself,
      rotten, no good, shitty, failure,
      dissolved in my tears,
my tears poured out of me in my dream and I wept
for my brother and wept when I turned after he left
      and I reached for my sister and she was having coffee
with a friend—
      I wept in my dream because she was not available for me
when I needed her,
and all my tears flowed, and how I wept, my feeling my pain
      of abandonment,
      all my tears became that arc of water
      and I became the flower, by sheer accident in the middle
      of nowhere, blossoming . . .

Twenty-eight

Over my shoulder
      the days blow like yellow leaves. It's hard to keep
them fresh. Already, my memories are put away, folded like a child's
pajamas, in an empty room in my heart. I ponder on this room,
a parent wondering of his children, grown up, faded into natural lives;
I stand at the door, thinking maybe I could have done something
      different.
      Maybe I will stand here the rest of my life,
      maybe the answer is here, in what was;
      there is no contentment.
      I open the blinds, let sunshine flood the floor.
      Sometimes I'll sit in the dark and think,
      think, and think. It hasn't been a peaceful life.
      These memories, once set out to conquer like kings,
      were subdued by the beauty of women,
      frightened by today's savage civility,
      too weak to climb, seeking something indestructible
      to stand upon and make a life of their own.

      And at times when unexpectedly they burst
      through doors into my house and find me thinking,
      we embrace, we share the night locked in pain
      and love, like escaped convicts
      they leave before I awake. I turn over in bed,
      mourning their departure, fearing their capture.

Twenty-nine

This poem is a prayer candle
lit twenty years ago one night
when life seemed so lonely, a forsaken place,
and the world an altar I knelt at
with bums and addicts in gutters
dying in the dark freezing night,
children weeping with stark cries of hopelessness,
when faith in the heart of man seemed to abandon
each soul, leaving it open like an ugly wound,
a shattered door the occupant destroyed and pillaged,
leaving only pained howlings of people
blind to their brothers' and sisters' suffering—
and it was twenty years ago this night
that wings of a divine presence
lifted me from my own despair,
brushed ashes of grief from my shoulders
and gave me the gift to see beyond my own pain—
blessed me with empathy and compassion—
my soul like an old stick to find water in the ground,
twisted brittle leafless soul shivered me toward
the mystery of my breathing,
leading me back across the wasteland of my life
to marvel at my own experience and those around me
whose own humble lives graced me with assurance
that if I stayed on the path of love, of seeking the good in people,
of trying to be an honorable man,
that I too would one day have the love of family and friends
and be a part of life as it spun like a star in the dark
radiating light on its journey—

and there is one thing I know with certainty—
that there is a great power within us, that when used in purity,
unselfishness and immaculate thought,
cures, heals and causes miracles
and now assists me in my journey—
and this gift given me twenty years ago
I now give back
as a poem, as a candle kept lit,
through all the tears and sadnesses,
sometimes unattended and barely giving any light
but always letting go its light as I let go
in giving and compassion for others,
sharing it with others
in the night,
to those who dream for peace,
for those who cherish the light, pass it on.